RABBITS

Alvin and Virginia Silverstein
RABBITS
All About Them

with photographs by **Roger Kerkham**

Lothrop, Lee & Shepard Company / New York

Acknowledgments

The authors would like to thank Roger and Betty Kerkham for their enthusiastic support; Dr. T. D. Luckey and Dr. Philip Schain for their kind help and interest in the project; and Snuffy, Flopsy, Bun-Bun, Snooks, Carmen, and all the other long-eared friends who cooperated so amiably in the undertaking.

Silverstein, Alvin.
    Rabbits: all about them.

    SUMMARY: Examines the kinds and characteristics of rabbits, their care as pets, their role in legend and lore, their history, ecological importance, and usefulness in the laboratory.
    Includes bibliographical references.
    1. Rabbits—Juvenile literature. 2. Hares—Juvenile literature. [1. Rabbits. 2. Hares] I. Silverstein, Virginia B., joint author. II. Kerkham, Roger, illus. III. Title.
ꞁ QL737.L32S54 c/2 599'.322 ·   73-4952

ISBN 0-688-41564-4
ISBN 0-688-51564-9 (lib. bdg.)

For Nancy, Robert, Milissa, Sharon, and Allison Zwolinski

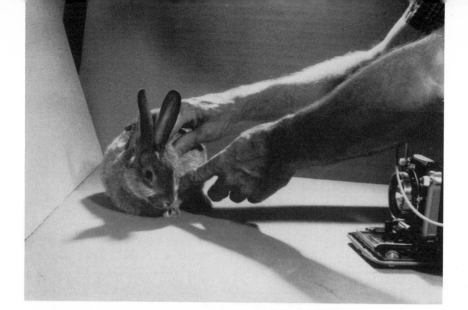

RABBITS

Contents

About Rabbits

The perfect gift for Easter? A rabbit, of course! Soft and cuddly, hardy and affectionate, these lovable animals are ideal pets all year round.

Rabbits were not always called "rabbits." They used to be called "conies." The name "rabbit" comes from a French word that was first used only for the young conies. Gradually the word came to be used for the adults as well.

The story of rabbits goes back a long time. Fossils of several kinds of rabbits, very similar to those living today, date back to about thirty million years ago. Paintings in caves in Spain, made during the Stone Age, show pictures of rabbits and hares. These pictures show that men were familiar with rabbits long before the time of written history, and probably used them for food and clothing.

The first written records of rabbits tell how ancient Phoenician traders, who sailed to Spain around 1000 B.C., picked up some rabbits and carried them to other countries around the Mediterranean. A giant statue of a sphinx, built in Turkey around 1500 B.C., stands on the figures of two rabbits, which shows that these animals were already known there at that time.

The ancient Romans liked to hunt rabbits and were very fond of their meat. They began to raise rabbits in walled enclosures and took them along to the countries they conquered. Soon the rabbits had spread all over Europe, and indeed, were doing so well that in some places they became pests, eating the farmers' crops. In England, Queen

Elizabeth I raised rabbits as pets and started a rabbit-raising fad among the nobles of her court.

English settlers took rabbits to Australia and New Zealand, where they thrived so well that they became a multiplying nightmare. The other continents have their own rabbitlike creatures living in fields and forests, deserts and Arctic wastes. And in all the civilized countries of today's world, rabbits are raised as pets, laboratory animals, and food animals.

Kinds of Rabbits

The wild rabbits that live in Europe, Africa, and Australia are small, long-eared animals with soft grayish-brown fur

This rabbit breed is called English Spot.

coats. Occasionally a rabbit with black or white fur will be found among them. Over the centuries, rabbit breeders have taken these unusual varieties and developed over fifty different breeds from them. Some are as large as spaniels, others as small as guinea pigs. Rabbits come in pure white, black, and a variety of distinctive colors and markings.

The Flemish giants are the largest of all the domestic rabbits. They may weigh 15 pounds or more, and their fur can be white or a variety of colors like gray or sandy.

A tiny rabbit with shiny white fur is the Polish rabbit. It may weigh less than 3 pounds when full grown.

Just as tiny is the Netherland Dwarf. This short-eared little rabbit may be a variety of colors. It is believed that the first Netherland Dwarfs came from Holland, where a Polish rabbit was accidentally crossed with a small wild rabbit.

The Netherland Dwarf is a tiny rabbit.

Dutch rabbits make good pets.

Another small rabbit (about 4 or 5 pounds) is the Dutch. This two-toned rabbit is black, gray, tan, or brown behind and on the head, with a broad belt of white fur around his middle and a blaze of white on his face. Dutch rabbits are popular pets and have charming dispositions.

Himalayan and Californian rabbits are white with black feet, noses, and ears. Together with New Zealand white rabbits, they are among the most popular rabbits raised for meat. Rabbit meat is especially high in protein and one of the most nutritious of all meats.

California (top) and New Zealand rabbits are often raised for meat.

Champagne d'argent rabbits change color as they grow.

Champagne d'argent rabbits are one of the oldest breeds. Their name means "silver rabbits from Champagne" (a province in France). Champagne d'argent babies are pure black, but their fur lightens gradually to silver as they grow.

This French Angora rabbit has had a haircut.

Angora rabbits have long, silky fur and come in various colors. (The white ones are the most popular.) Their long hair can be clipped and sold.

Lop-eared rabbits have enormous, drooping ears that may be up to 15 inches long and 7 inches wide.

Belgian hares are long and lanky. They are among the most intelligent of all rabbits.

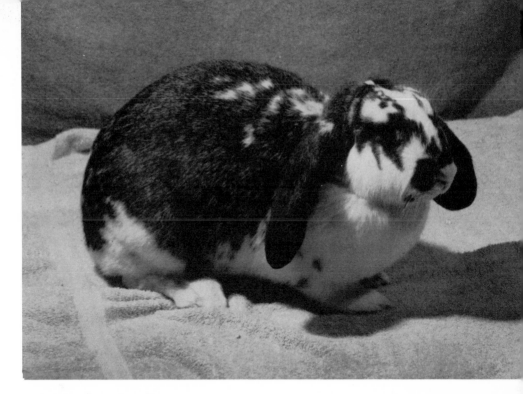

French lops have long floppy ears.

Belgian hares are long and lanky.

Rabbit Relatives

For a long time it was thought that rabbits and their long-eared relatives, the hares, belonged to the group of rodents. Rats and mice are rodents, as are guinea pigs, squirrels, gophers, beavers, and porcupines.

Like the rodents, rabbits and hares have very large, long front teeth, or incisors. These front teeth keep growing throughout the animal's entire life. He must constantly gnaw on things—firm roots and twigs, for example—to keep his incisors worn down. If a rabbit or a rodent does not have enough gnawing food, his teeth will grow so long that he will be unable to close his mouth!

Yet a rabbit's teeth are not *exactly* like those of a mouse or a guinea pig. Rodents have only four front teeth, two on top and two on the bottom. Rabbits and hares have an extra, smaller, pair of upper incisors, one on each side of the two large front ones.

Buck teeth and a harelip.

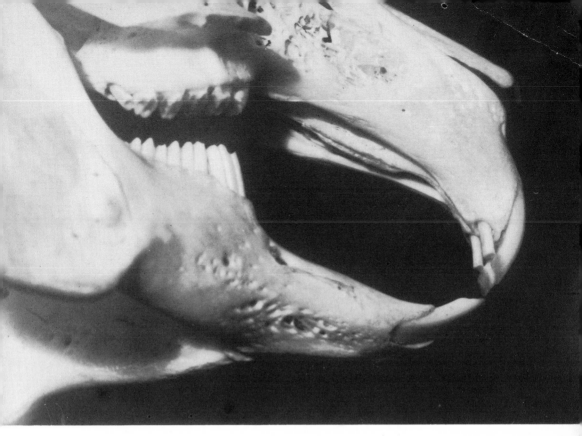

Rabbits and hares have two extra top incisors.

After the incisors, in both rabbits and hares, and in rodents, there is a large empty space called a "diastema." It looks almost as though some teeth have fallen out. But no teeth ever grow in this gap during the animal's whole life.

Behind the diastema, at the back of the jaws, are the premolars and molars, the grinding teeth. These teeth look very similar in rabbits and in rodents, but they use them differently. Rodents chew their food with back and forth grinding motions. But rabbits and hares move their jaws from side to side as they chew. There is a good reason for this. A rabbit's lower jaw is much narrower than his upper jaw. So there is no way that all his molars can

23

meet at the same time. When the upper and lower molars on the right side are lined up, the left molars do not meet. He must move his lower jaw to the side to line up his left molars—and then the right ones no longer meet.

There are other differences, too. Rabbits and hares have deeply slit upper lips (harelips) that show their upper incisors clearly even when their mouths are closed. They have long, sensitive ears, which they can turn like antennas to gather in sounds.

Long ears like antennas.

A rabbit's hind legs are longer than his forelegs.

Rabbits and hares do not walk and run the way most other animals do. If you have ever watched a cat or dog walking, you may have noticed that it picks up one foot at a time in turn, always leaving three feet on the ground. In running, the second foot is picked up before the first is back on the ground. But the two feet on the ground are always in a certain combination: a front foot on one side and a hind foot on the other. And all four legs are about the same length. Rabbits and hares have hind legs that are much longer and stronger than their forelegs. They bound along, propelling themselves forward with powerful thrusts

25

of their hind legs and using the front legs to keep their bodies balanced. Both hind feet hit the ground at the same time. A rabbit's tracks look curious. The prints of its big hind feet are in *front* of the prints of its forepaws. The faster it is going, the longer the space between the two sets of prints.

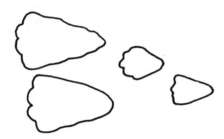

Snowshoe rabbit

Black-tailed jack rabbit

Cottontail rabbit

(moving from right to left in all cases)

Rabbits and hares are vegetarians.

Many rodents, such as mice and squirrels, can turn their forepaws inward and use them like hands. A squirrel holds a nut in its paw as it nibbles away. A rabbit or hare cannot hold things in its paws. If it wants to carry something —a bundle of grass, perhaps, or a baby—it must use its mouth.

Another difference of the rabbits and hares is in their digestive system. These animals are vegetarians, and plant foods are very hard to digest. Plant cells are bound in a tough substance called cellulose, which locks in the nutrients they contain. The cellulose must be broken down before an animal can get all the nourishment in plant foods.

27

Several different things contribute to the success of rabbits and hares in living on plant foods. First of all, their digestive system is unusually long. If the digestive system of a little 15 inch rabbit were stretched out to its full length, it would measure more than 20 feet! (The digestive system of a 6-foot man is only about 30 feet long.)

In addition, rabbits and hares have a special fold in a part of their intestines called the caecum. Bacteria that are able to break down cellulose live there. They are like courteous guests who help their hosts to digest the food they eat. Even vegetarian rodents, such as guinea pigs, do not have the special fold in their caecum.

Rabbits and hares have a habit that aids them still more in digesting their vegetable diet. They eat their food twice! The first time, the undigested food passes out of the body in the form of soft, moist droppings. Before one of these pellets has a chance to drop off, the rabbit or hare snatches it in its mouth and swallows it. Now it has another chance to digest the food, and in addition, it has picked up a generous helping of extra vitamins, which the bacteria in its intestines have produced. Rodents generally do not eat their droppings this way.

With all these differences, many scientists felt uneasy about calling rabbits and hares rodents. They thought that perhaps these animals should be put in a different group, called "lagomorphs" (from words meaning "harelike"). The final piece of evidence came from a modern scientific technique.

Blood serum, the liquid part of blood, contains a number of different chemicals. Some of these are proteins, and many of them are different for each kind of animal. Blood also contains a part of the body's disease-fighting system, special cells that can recognize chemicals that are foreign, or different from the body's normal chemicals. When a foreign chemical invades the bloodstream, the body's disease-fighting cells produce antibodies, which attack the strange chemical. This system is very useful in fighting invading bacteria, which are covered with foreign chemicals. It also works against any sort of chemical that is not normal to the body.

If blood from, let us say, a guinea pig, is injected into the blood vessels of a horse, the horse's body will produce antibodies against all the chemicals that are special for guinea pigs, but not against the proteins that both horses and guinea pigs share. The more closely two kinds of animals are related, the more chemicals they have in common, and the fewer antibodies will be produced in such a blood-serum test.

When blood-serum tests were developed, scientists tried them out with rabbits to see which animals were their closest relatives. They injected rabbit blood into a guinea pig. The guinea pig's body made antibodies against all the rabbit blood chemicals that were foreign to it. Now the guinea pig blood contained a sort of "anti-rabbit serum." When samples of this anti-rabbit serum were mixed with samples of rabbit blood, the antibodies reacted with the rabbit blood chemicals, and a solid substance, or precipitate, was formed. If samples of anti-rabbit serum were mixed with the blood of other animals, a certain amount of precipitate was formed also, though not as much as with rabbit blood. The more chemicals the other animal shared in common with rabbits—that is, the more closely related they were—the more of the precipitate would be formed. Imagine the scientists' surprise when blood-serum tests showed that rabbits are not very closely related to rodents at all. Indeed, they are much more closely related to the hoofed mammals, such as pigs, cows, and horses.

With all this evidence, it was decided to place the rabbits and hares, together with some curious little animals called pikas, in a separate group called "Lagomorpha."

Rabbits and guinea pigs get along well together, but they are not very closely related.

Rabbits as Pets

Would you like a pet who is easy to care for and doesn't need much room or very expensive food? who is clean and gentle and affectionate? who loves to play and be petted and will follow you around like a puppy? If you would, a rabbit is just the pet for you.

Choosing a Rabbit

If you live in a rural area, it is likely that someone you know raises rabbits and might give or sell you one. In the city, you can get a rabbit at a pet shop. You will find the largest selection just before Easter. There are more than fifty different kinds to choose from—short-haired rabbits and long, fluffy-haired angoras; white rabbits and black ones; gray and brown and blue and buffy tan; spotted

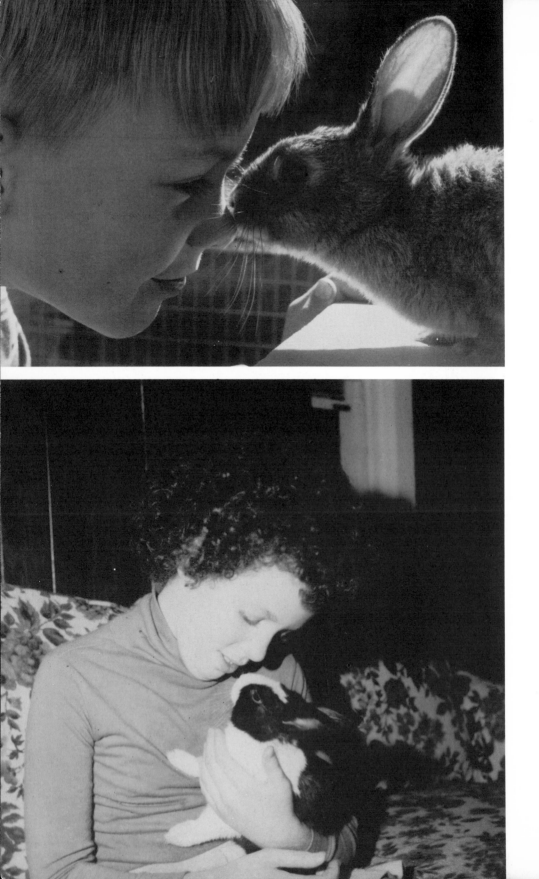

rabbits and belted Dutch rabbits; big rabbits and small ones; and rabbits with long floppy ears. Pick the one that suits you best.

When you choose a rabbit, be sure to pick one that is bright-eyed and active. Its fur should be clean and shiny. Matter fur and stains on its underparts may mean that it has diarrhea. Then you would find yourself with a sick rabbit who might even die after you took him home. Try to get a young rabbit, two or three months old. If he is given a great deal of handling and affection by humans early in his life, he will be a much tamer and more loving pet.

Should you get one rabbit or two or more? There are several things to consider. One, of course, is how much room you have, and where you are going to keep your rabbits. Another is the fact that rabbits are very sociable animals. If you have only one rabbit, you must be prepared to give it a lot of love and attention, and it will be very affectionate to you in turn.

For a while we had only one rabbit, a little black-and-white Dutch rabbit named Snuffy. He had the run of the house, and there were times when we wondered whether he really knew he was a rabbit. He played with the cats (he loved to creep up behind them and nibble at their tails) and he seemed to prefer their cat food to his own rabbit pellets. If a human came into the room, he would hop up to be sociable. Sometimes he would hop around and around us in a circle for minutes at a time. We would get tired of the game long before he would. And if anyone

Rabbit day in school.

happened to be sitting down, he would hop up onto the person's lap to be patted.

But rabbits are such sociable animals that they are really happier with others of their kind. When we finally brought home a bride for Snuffy, he was overjoyed. He ran to her immediately, and for the next whole week he followed her around like a shadow. He never let her alone for a minute. Poor Flopsy, the doe, was a little upset by the whole situation. She had been born and raised in an outdoor hutch on a rabbit farm, and she was not accustomed to all the attention and to living in a house with people. She kept crawling under the furniture, trying to escape from Snuffy and from the children, who wanted to pet both of them. Eventually she did get used to all of us, and after the novelty of discovering the rabbit world wore off, Snuffy became his old affectionate self.

Carmen and Snooks are the best of friends.

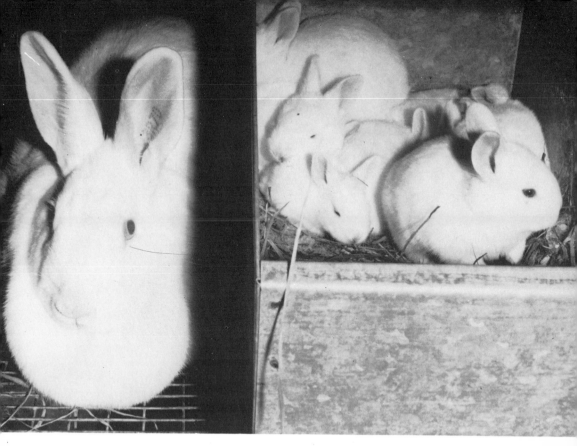

A nest box of her own.

You can raise two male rabbits together only if there are no females around. Otherwise they will fight, and must be separated. Two females will also get along well. If you want to breed rabbits and raise their young, of course, you must start with both a buck and a doe. They will be quite content with each other; like their wild ancestors, domestic rabbits may mate for life. But, also like male rabbits in the wilds, a domestic buck will be just as happy with several does as his mates. The does do not seem to mind this arrangement, as long as each can raise her family in a nest box of her own.

37

Homes for Rabbits

Before we had our first rabbits, we raised guinea pigs for many years and found that we could house them quite nicely in a large cardboard box with newspaper spread on the bottom. When we tried a similar arrangement with rabbits, we found it was not at all satisfactory—unless you do not mind finding rabbits all over the house. They jump right out of the box.

So, when you bring your pet rabbit home, you must quickly decide where and how you are going to keep him.

One possibility is simply to let the rabbit go wherever he pleases. You can leave his food and water dishes in some convenient place (be sure the door of that room is never closed so that he cannot get to his supplies) and set up a little bed or nest box for him. However, you will prob-

A rabbit on the loose can find all sorts of interesting things to play with.

Other family pets get along with rabbits.

ably find him ignoring his nest and sleeping up on some-body's bed instead.

There are a number of advantages to letting a pet rabbit run free in the house. He has an opportunity to become a real member of the family that way. He is always around to be petted and played with. He will enjoy playing with the children's toys and may even watch television with the family. Other pets, such as cats and dogs, quickly get used to him and learn that he is not to be bothered. Kittens and puppies will play with a rabbit just as though he were another of their own kind.

One of them is a bit confused.

But there are some important disadvantages to giving a pet rabbit the run of the house. One is the messes he makes. If you are patient, you can solve that problem by teaching him to use a litter box, like a cat. Rabbits are naturally clean animals, and if you place some of your rabbit's droppings in the litter box, he may soon get the idea.

Another possible problem is that you must be careful not to let him slip outside when you open the door. Since he is tame, he will not go far—just scamper around a bit to enjoy the fresh air. But if you do not realize he is out, he may be in danger from prowling cats or dogs. To strangers' dogs or cats, he is just a rabbit, not your pet rabbit.

Still another possible disadvantage is that when you don't know exactly where your rabbit is all the time, he may be stepped on accidentally. But the most serious of all comes from a part of the rabbit's nature that neither you nor he can do anything about.

Rabbits, like rodents, have front teeth that continue to grow all their lives. They have a continual need to chew on things; they *must* do so in order to keep their teeth worn down to a manageable size. They will chew on anything that seems suitable. A hint of the difficulties that can arise with rabbits running loose was found in a report that our son Glenn once wrote for school: "Rabbits chew on things. So if you have rabbits keep your Important things in a safe

Paper is for chewing.

place and do not let the rabbit or rabbits in the room that you put your papers in."

We generally provided our rabbits with branches and twigs to chew on and never had any problems with gnawed furniture legs. But when we discovered half the insulation chewed off the vacuum-cleaner cord (fortunately it was not plugged in!), we knew our rabbits would have to be confined.

Suppliers for rabbit breeders sell all-wire rabbit hutches that are roomy and easy to keep clean. But you can build a hutch that is quite satisfactory with some wood and wire mesh. The hutch should be at least 2 by 2 by 3 feet, to give the rabbit some room in which to move around. The sides and top should be wire screening, and the bottom may also

Some designs for indoor hutches.

The hutches below have no bottoms. They are placed on a hay-covered shelf.

be wire mesh (about ½-inch mesh is good). A hutch with a mesh floor is easier to keep clean, for the rabbit's droppings fall right through. You can keep a tray or a spread-out newspaper underneath and dispose of them easily. (They make excellent fertilizer for a garden.) Some breeds of rabbits need a wood floor. A hutch with a solid floor must be scraped out and cleaned thoroughly at least once or twice a week.

In either case, your rabbit should have some soft bedding to lie on. Hay is the best, but shredded newspaper, straw, or peat moss will do nicely. The bedding should be changed every few days.

Hay is good for burrowing, playing, and eating.

Even in a cage a rabbit can have lots of fun with such toys as a paper bag . . . a can with a stone in it to rattle . . .

a crackerbox playhouse . . .

It is a good idea to enclose a small area of the hutch with wooden walls, with a canvas flap for a door, so that the rabbit will have a private "bedroom" to retire to. A wooden box with a doorway cut out of it will be satisfactory. Even a cardboard box will do, but you must be prepared to replace it frequently, as the rabbit chews it to pieces.

It is not wise to enclose the whole hutch. Rabbits can stand the cold much better than they can stand heat, and

46

and a card board tunnel.

they need plenty of ventilation. If you have more than one rabbit, it is best to have a separate hutch for each.

Outdoor Living

Many rabbit breeders raise their rabbits outdoors all year round. Rabbits are hardy animals, and they thrive through the winter even in a screen-walled hutch. If you build an outdoor hutch, be sure to provide a roof with an overhang

Outdoor hutches.

to shield the rabbits from the sun and weather. Canvas flaps on the sides, which can be lowered for extra protection, are also a good idea. The wire mesh of an outdoor hutch should be no wider than ½-inch mesh. That will keep the hutch free of mice and keep the neighborhood cats from sticking their claws in.

Many rabbit breeders combine two profitable hobbies. They place boxes of soil under the mesh floors of their rabbit hutches and grow earthworms in them. The rabbit droppings fertilize the soil and help to feed the earthworms, which can be sold for fishing bait and for use in scientific laboratories.

These earthworms live in the soil under a rabbit hutch.

Enjoying the outdoors.

If you keep your rabbit indoors, you will want to take him outside for exercise when the weather is nice. Don't take him out on very cold days. Although rabbits can live through the winter easily when they have had a chance to get used to the cold gradually, they may be chilled if they have been used to living in a heated room.

You can take a rabbit for walks on a leash like a dog. You should use a figure-eight cat harness rather than a collar around his neck, so that you will not choke him.

A rabbit will enjoy the exercise of daily walks, but he will have even more fun if you can let him run free in an enclosed pen. He can nibble at the grass and sniff the fresh air and hop about. The fence should be at least four feet high, and the mesh should be narrow enough (about 1 inch).

When we first moved to the country, we decided to ac-

50

complish two purposes at once by putting our rabbits out during the day in the play yard we built on the front lawn for our two youngest children. Laura and Kevin thought it was a marvelous idea. The only problem was that an hour or so after putting two children and four rabbits into the pen, we would come back to find only two children and *two* rabbits inside. The mesh of the fence was about 2 inches, which was enough to told in the two larger rabbits (Flemish and Angora). But though our two little Dutch rabbits looked much fatter than two inches, they still managed to get out. We caught them at it a few times, and it was fascinating to watch. They seemed to melt right through the wire. We never did figure out how they did it, but they led us a merry chase. Fortunately they usually made for a hollow tree nearby and were easily recaptured.

We eventually built the rabbits a pen of their own, with a narrower mesh fence, but our problems were not over. The rabbits learned how to climb over the fence! Our children unwittingly helped them: they climbed into the pen to play with the rabbits so often that they dented the wire down in several places. After chasing rabbits for half

This outdoor pen is big enough for a child and a rabbit.

the summer, we finally locked them up in an outdoor hutch and took them out only under strict supervision.

Feeding

Pet shops and animal-supply houses sell rabbit foods in the form of small dry pellets. These prepared foods contain alfalfa meal, barley, oats, corn, wheat, and supplements of vitamins and minerals. They provide the rabbits with a balanced diet of the foods that are best for them, in a form that is easy to store and feed. Most breeders advise feeding rabbits once or twice a day, being careful not to let them overeat and develop a fat potbelly. A mother rabbit who is raising a litter of young needs to have a supply of food available at all times. The feed should be placed in a heavy crock. Rabbits can be clumsy, and may knock over a light dish and spill their food.

Feed rabbit pellets in a dish the rabbits can't knock over.

Fastening the water bowl above the floor helps keep it clean. Little Snooks (right) can reach the bowl if she wants to.

In addition to rabbit pellets, rabbits need a supply of fresh water. You can use a special watering bottle or place the water in another heavy crock. If you do give your rabbit water in an open bowl, be sure to change the water and clean the bowl at least once a day.

The commercial rabbit pellets contain all the nourishment your rabbit needs, but he will enjoy having some other foods as treats. Some hay to munch on helps to add some bulk in his diet. Fresh-cut grass, dandelion greens,

Carrots are a special treat.

lettuce and cabbage leaves are welcome changes. Carrots, both the tops and the roots, are a special delight. Milk to drink, or whole-grain bread soaked in milk is also good for rabbits, especially nursing mothers. Your rabbit will also appreciate your hanging a small salt block in his hutch for him to nibble at. It is round with a hole in the middle, and you can get it at a pet shop.

54

Most people who raise rabbits never realize that these animals eat some of their food twice. Like their lagomorph relatives, tame rabbits reingest, or "re-eat," soft, moist pellets that have already passed through their digestive system. But they usually do this early in the morning, when no one is looking at them.

It is easy to train a rabbit to stand up for his food.

Hold a rabbit so that he feels secure.

Caring for Rabbits

If you want your rabbit to be friendly and loving, you must handle him a great deal. The more gentle care you give him, the tamer he will become. Always pick him up gently but firmly, giving him a feeling of support. A rabbit's ears are not handles. Never pick him up by the ears! The proper way to pick up a rabbit is to lift him by the

56

skin at the nape of the neck with one hand, while holding the other hand under his hind quarters. Always use two hands, and hold him close to your body. If he feels insecure or is pulled about roughly, he may struggle and scratch, or even bite.

You need not worry too much about being soiled by a rabbit while you are holding it. Rabbits do not usually urinate while they are being held, and their droppings are in the form of hard little pellets, which can easily be scooped up and thrown away, leaving no stain or odor.

Unless you have an Angora rabbit, you will not have to do anything to keep your rabbit clean and neat. He will do

Rabbits are clean animals and learn to wash themselves at an early age.

the job himself. He licks his fur just like a housecat and keeps himself clean and shining from his nose to his tail. An Angora rabbit may need some extra help to keep his long silky fur brushed free of dirt and tangles.

Rabbits are generally healthy animals, if their quarters are kept clean and well ventilated and they are fed properly.

An Angora needs more care.

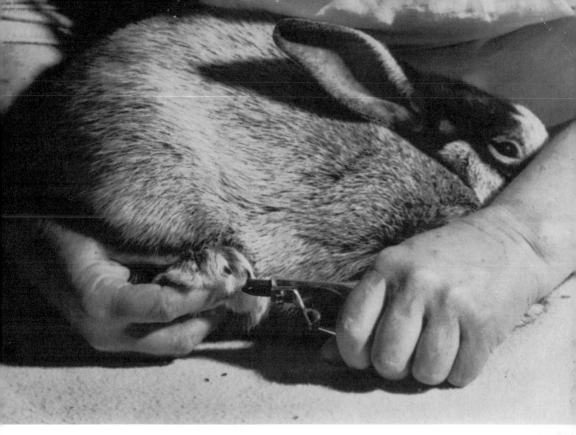

The tips of a rabbit's toenails may need clipping.

Occasionally a rabbit may catch a cold, with sneezing and a runny nose that make him just as miserable as humans are when they have a cold. Usually he will recover by himself if he is kept warm and dry.

Too many fresh greens in a rabbit's diet may give him diarrhea. The treatment for this is to cut out the fresh greens for a while and give him dry food, with some hay or straw if possible. A little drained boiled rice may help sometimes.

If you notice that your rabbit seems to be shaking his head frequently or scratching at his ear, he may have an ear infection called ear canker. This can be treated by

59

This rabbit has a dewlap on her neck. No one knows quite what causes it, but it does not mean that she is sick.

wiping out the ear with hydrogen peroxide (about a tea-spoonful to a cup of warm water), then dropping in a few drops of vegetable oil or an ear ointment for cats.

If you notice that your rabbit has fleas, treat them right

away with a flea preparation for cats. Because rabbits lick their fur, as cats do, never use any preparation designed for dogs on them—it might be poisonous. Be sure to change the rabbit's bedding and clean his hutch thoroughly. If you do not solve the flea problem early, these little pests may spread through the house and give you flea bites, too.

If these simple remedies do not help or if your rabbit seems very sick, you should take him to a veterinarian.

Breeding Rabbits

Many jokes have been made about how rabbits multiply. If you want to have the fun of watching babies grow, rabbits are good animals to work with.

If you are letting your rabbits run free, or keeping a buck and a doe together in one large hutch, you will not have to worry about what to do to breed them. The rabbits will take care of that as soon as they are old enough. A doe can be bred at about five to eight months, depending on her breed. (Rabbits of small breeds mature faster than large ones.) If you do plan to breed your rabbit, you should not wait too long after she is mature. Rabbits' bones get harder as they get older. If the bones around a doe's birth canal harden before she has had her first litter, they may leave an opening so narrow that she will have difficulty if she has a litter later.

If you are keeping each rabbit in a separate hutch, you will need to bring them together in order for them to mate. Always place the doe in the buck's hutch, and not the other way around. The doe considers her hutch her home territory, and she will not allow strangers in it. She will attack the buck, and may even injure him before she has a chance to learn to know and like him.

In some ways, the mating of rabbits is rather unusual. Like most other mammals, a female has an "estrus cycle," or regular periods of "heat," when she is ready and willing to mate. Her cycle covers about sixteen days. Unlike most female mammals, who can mate only during a very short period of each cycle, a rabbit doe will accept a buck's attentions through all but a few days of her cycle. So it is likely that your rabbits will be ready to mate no matter when you bring them together—and if not, you need only to wait a few days and try again.

If the doe is willing, she will crouch quietly and permit the buck to mount her. After mating, he often will comically fall over onto his side. During mating, the buck has placed his sperm, the male sex cells, inside the doe's body. Now something unusual happens.

Female mammals produce their sex cells, the eggs, or ova, in a pair of organs called ovaries. At regular periods,

The fun of watching babies grow.

Some rabbits do not get very large when they are pregnant. This is Bun-Bun just a few days before kindling.

one or more ova are released from the ovaries and travel to the womb, where the young will develop. If the female has mated during this time, sperm from the male will join with her eggs and form one or more babies. If she has not mated at the right time, the ova pass out of her body, and no new lives are started.

In rabbits, ova are not released until *after* mating. The act of mating itself seems to stimulate the release of the ova, and thus helps to make sure that babies will be conceived. If the buck and doe are left together after mating, they will continue to mate from time to time all through her pregnancy, although no new babies will be conceived.

Rabbits give birth to a litter about thirty days after mating. At first you will not notice anything different about the doe, but as the weeks go by, her belly will gradually grow larger and begin to stick out on the sides. After a while, you will sometimes see little ripples under the skin of her belly, as her growing babies move and kick inside her. As the time of the birth approaches, you should be sure to provide a clean, dry nest box for her. A week or so before she is due to "kindle," or give birth, the doe will begin to pull soft fur from her belly to line the nest. Not only will her babies have a soft bed to lie in, but in pulling out the fur she exposes her eight nipples so that it will be easier for them to drink.

Bun-Bun waited until the last day to build a nest for her first litter.

It is better to let the doe alone while she is kindling. If you try to help her, you may make her nervous and upset, and she may even kill her young. Indeed, you should let the nest box alone for a few days after the birth. If you do look at the babies, do so while the doe is away from the nest. You can distract her attention with a tempting treat of her favorite food. Be careful not to let any bright lights shine on the babies, for their eyes are very sensitive at first.

The mother rabbit usually has from six to ten in a litter, although she may have more. The all-time record is twenty-three. If you breed two does at the same time, and one has a much larger litter than the other, you can give some of the extra babies to the mother with a smaller litter. If this is done during the first two days, she will raise these babies like her own.

When rabbits are first born, they have no fur at all. Their eyes and ears are sealed shut, and they are completely helpless. All they can do is drink their mother's milk. The mother rabbit generally feeds her babies for only a

Bun-Bun's babies two days old.

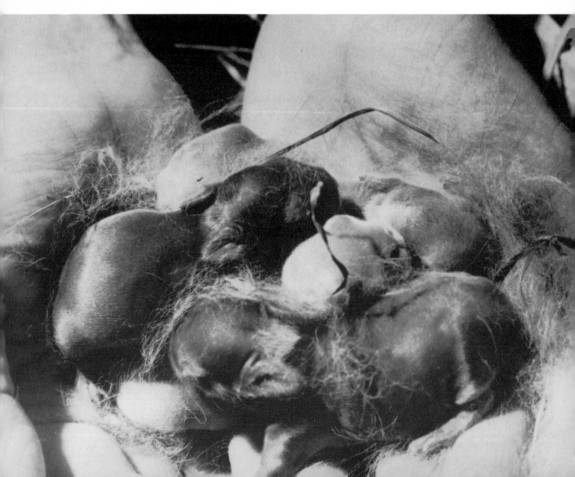

The babies lie on their backs to nurse.

few minutes, once or twice a day. Yet her milk is so rich that the young rabbits grow quickly. Within a few days they are covered with fuzz, and by two weeks or so they have a full coat of fur. By this time their eyes are fully opened, and they can hold their ears up straight. Their ears still seem very short in proportion to their bodies. Soon they begin to hop out of the nest box and nibble at their mother's rabbit pellets. But normally they are not weaned until they are six to eight weeks old.

After the young rabbits are weaned, they can be fed rabbit pellets, milk diluted with an equal amount of water,

One day old.

See how the little rabbit grows. Each square is one inch.

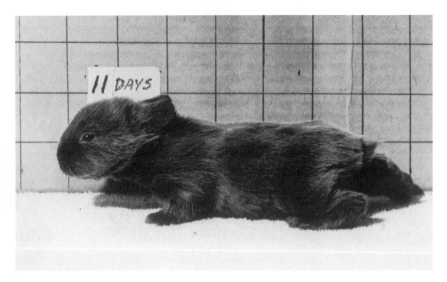

Eleven days old.

Twenty days old.

Twenty-eight days old.

Seven weeks old.

and a vitamin supplement. They should not be fed much greens until they are about four months old, as they may develop a potbelly or diarrhea.

Experienced rabbit breeders can determine the sex of rabbits when they are as young as one day old. But it is much easier to tell the sex of a rabbit after a few weeks.

69

To sex a young rabbit, hold it on its back, gently but firmly. Holding its tail back with the index finger of one hand, press gently beside its sex organs with your thumbs. If it is male, its sex organ will poke out as a tiny rounded tip. If it is a female, its sex organ will look like a slit, depressed a bit toward the rear. Don't do this too often with the same young rabbit, as you may hurt it.

Sexing rabbits.

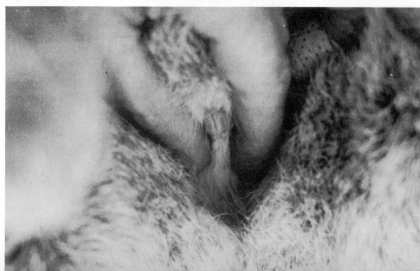

About a month after Flopsy had her first litter of eight, we discovered why most breeders recommend that the buck should not be left with the doe when she is expecting a litter. She suddenly presented us with another litter of thirteen! Apparently Snuffy had discovered she had given birth to her first litter before we did. All the babies of the second litter seemed healthy, and Flopsy raised them successfully, but it is not considered a good idea to rebreed a doe immediately too often. Having so many litters in so short a time is a great strain on her, and her health may suffer.

If you raise your rabbits indoors, they may breed all year round. In outdoor hutches, they may not breed during the winter, and if they do, the babies may die in the unheated hutches.

Sometimes a doe may appear to be pregnant and even build a nest and pull fur from her belly—yet time goes by and she does not kindle. She may be having a false pregnancy. This can be stimulated by the presence of bucks in nearby hutches, or it may occur when one doe mounts another. In other cases, a buck and a doe may mate, yet no litter is born. This happens especially often with very young does. It is a carryover from the wild rabbit ancestors. Under the uncertain conditions of the wilds, rabbits may mate and then the weather may change, or pressure from predators or overcrowding may make it almost certain that a little could not survive. If this happens or the doe is upset, the babies developing inside her may suddenly die and be absorbed back into her body. After this process is complete, there is not a trace that she was pregnant, and she may go on to mate and have another litter if conditions become more favorable. Flopsy did not have her first litter until about three months after she first met Snuffy. Possibly she was too young to mate successfully at first, or she may have reabsorbed a litter or two.

If you plan to show your rabbits, you will want to be sure to breed only rabbits of the same kind. But if you are raising rabbits just for fun, you may enjoy crossing two different breeds, to see what the young will look like. (Be careful never to breed a buck of a large breed to a doe of a small breed. She may have difficulty in kindling, and if the babies are too large, she may even die.) You will find that

At the rabbit and cavy show in Puyallup, Washington.

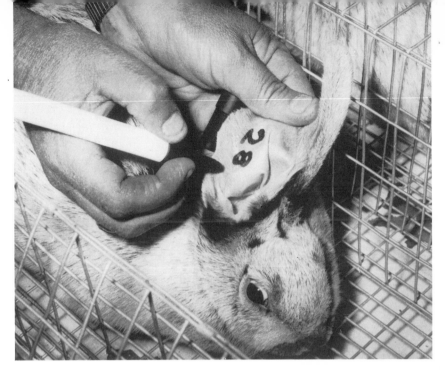

All the rabbits in the show are marked to identify them if they get loose. The numbers will come off in a few days.

The judge may offer some helpful hints to young rabbit raisers.

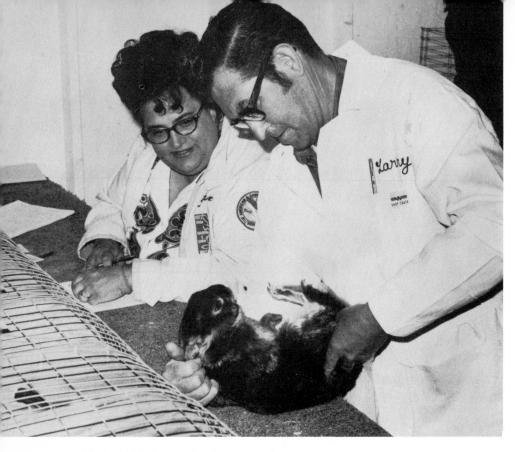

Each rabbit is examined very carefully.

These are the prizes waiting for the winners.

YOUTH TROPHY'S
D BY
IC SUPPLY · SEATTLE
AL WAY SUZUKI
EYERS CYCLE · RENTON

some traits are passed on from parent to child, while others may skip a generation, disappearing in the children but reappearing in the grandchildren.

For example, our Snuffy was a little black and white Dutch rabbit, while Flopsy was a Californian rabbit, with a white body, red eyes, and dark gray ears and nose. She also had a habit of holding one ear down unless she was especially listening for something, while Snuffy always hopped about with both ears erect. All the young of their litters had the typical Dutch markings, though some had

Snuffy, Flopsy, and one of their babies.

Flopsy usually held one ear down.

Bun-Bun and her first litter.

Bun-Bun's second brood had the same father. What happened?

more dark fur than others. Most were black and white, but a few in each litter were gray and white. And all the young rabbits held both ears up straight.

By cross-breeding rabbits and following traits like these, you may be able to discover for yourself some laws of heredity. And you may discover some unusually attractive rabbit varieties that you may ultimately develop into a brand-new breed.

Rabbits in the Laboratory

Many people owe their lives to rabbits. For rabbits are among the animals commonly used in the laboratory by scientists and doctors.

Rabbits have a number of advantages as laboratory animals. They are clean, gentle, and easy to care for. They are fairly large animals, and yet they do not take up too much room. They grow and mature quickly. And, of course, they multiply . . . like rabbits!

Rabbits are used in a variety of scientific investigations. Researchers use them to study the effects of drugs and radiations, and gain insights into the effects these agents may have on humans. They can test the effects of certain diets and food additives on rabbits. Rabbits are susceptible to many of the same diseases as humans, from diphtheria

Rabbits wait in a holding pen to be sent to laboratories all over the country.

to tuberculosis, smallpox, rabies, cancer, and even warts. Thus, they can be used to develop tests for these diseases; and new treatments can be tried out on rabbits before they are tried on humans.

These same sorts of studies can be run on a number of other species of animals as well, such as rats and mice, guinea pigs, dogs, and cats. But in many cases, rabbits are the "animal of choice," because of their size (they are much larger than mice, rats, and guinea pigs, and give scientists more blood or other materials to work with) and special similarities of their reactions to those of man.

79

Rabbit Tests

A famous test for pregnancy is called the "rabbit test." If a woman wishes to know whether she is pregnant, she brings a sample of her urine to a laboratory. Some of her urine may then be injected into an adult female rabbit who is not pregnant at the time. If the woman is really expecting a baby, her urine will contain a special hormone called "chorionic gonadotropin." This hormone can cause changes in the ovaries of a rabbit, causing some of the tiny sacs that hold ova to burst open. About two days after the injection, the technician examines the rabbit's ovaries. If these changes are there, the woman is pregnant; if not, she is not.

Rabbit tests have also been developed for a number of diseases. For example, both rabbits and humans are susceptible to diphtheria. In a test for diphtheria, one rabbit is given a dose of diphtheria antitoxin (a substance that counteracts the toxin or poison that diphtheria germs produce), while another is not. Then samples of wipings from the patient's throat are injected into the bellies of both rabbits. If the patient has a case of toxin-producing diphtheria, the rabbit protected by the antitoxin will have no reaction to the injection. But the unprotected rabbit will develop a large rash.

Rabbits are also susceptible to tuberculosis, particularly the kind that is transmitted in milk. Before milk was pasteurized, rabbits were specially bred for even greater susceptibility to tuberculosis. These special lines of rabbits were widely used in tests for TB and in developing treatments for the disease.

Rabbits are especially useful in the testing and study of the venereal disease syphilis. Syphilis microbes are difficult to study because they normally do not grow in any animals other than man. But they can grow in rabbits. If syphilis microbes are injected into the testes of a rabbit, these organs change the germs slightly, into a form that can be used in a test for syphilis antibodies.

In blood transfusions, a patient may have a serious reaction if his own blood contains chemicals that conflict with the chemicals in the blood that is given to him. Rabbits are used in blood-serum tests to determine possible conflicts.

Rabbits have rather sensitive skin, and they can be used to test whether a new face cream or ointment is likely to cause allergies. The fur is shaved off a patch of the rabbit's skin, and a sample of the cream is rubbed on. If the rabbit's skin develops a rash or redness, the researchers know that the cream might cause trouble for some humans also.

Rabbits' perky long ears suggested that they would be ideal animals for testing the effects of various drugs on cartilage. This is the tough gristly substance that helps to give the shape and firmness to various body parts, such as the nose and ears. It has been found that injections of the enzyme "papain" produce changes in the cartilage of rabbits' ears, causing them to droop. (Papain is the main ingredient in meat tenderizers. But tenderized steaks do not

In studies of steroid drugs, injections of papain made this rabbit's ears

droop. He will be back to normal in a few days.

cause people's ears to droop because the heat used to cook the steaks destroys the papain.) If the injections are stopped, the rabbits' ears soon recover and stand up straight again within a few days. But in one series of experiments it was found that steroid drugs, such as those used to treat arthritis, interfere with the recovery of cartilage. Rabbits given injections of papain and then steroids continued to have droopy ears until the steroid injections were stopped.

Rabbits also help to save people from horrible death from rabies. If a person is bitten by a mad dog or bat or other rabid animal, he is given a series of injections of rabies vaccine. This vaccine is prepared by injecting the rabies virus into rabbits, in whose bodies it multiplies and is changed slightly. When the patient is given larger and larger doses of the rabies virus from the rabbits' bodies, his own body gradually builds up protection against it.

Germfree Rabbits

Scientists in one field of research encountered some special problems when they tried to use rabbits in their investigations. These researchers were working in the field of germfree studies.

The world we live in is filled with germs. Microorganisms too small to see without a microscope swarm by the millions in air you breathe, in the water you drink, and on the ground you walk on. There are germs on every inch of your skin, no matter how carefully and often you bathe;

there are even germs inside your nose and mouth, your intestines, and other parts of your body. Some of these microorganisms can cause diseases. But most of them are simply part of the world we live in, and our bodies are able to get along with them without difficulty. In fact, some of the microorganisms that inhabit our inner and outer world can even be helpful. The bacteria in your intestines, for example, make more vitamins than they need for themselves, and your body absorbs and uses the excess.

About a century ago, it was discovered that germs can cause disease. Then it was natural for scientists to wonder what would happen if animals (and people) could be raised in an environment entirely free of germs. Would they be healthier, or would it be found that their bodies are so used to living in a world filled with microorganisms that they *need* germs to stay healthy?

It took many years of difficult and frustrating work before techniques were finally worked out to raise animals under completely germfree conditions. As the methods and instruments were perfected, rats and mice, dogs, cats, monkeys, chickens, sheep, pigs, and a variety of other animals were raised in airtight steel tanks or plastic film tents, completely separated from any contact with germs. But for many years, all the attempts to raise germfree rabbits were dismal failures. Few of the young rabbits born and raised under germfree conditions lived to maturity, and those that did were usually sickly and were unable to mate.

The main problem was that germfree rabbits quickly develop an enlarged caecum. This pouch in their intestines

The drawing below explains how this germfree tank works.

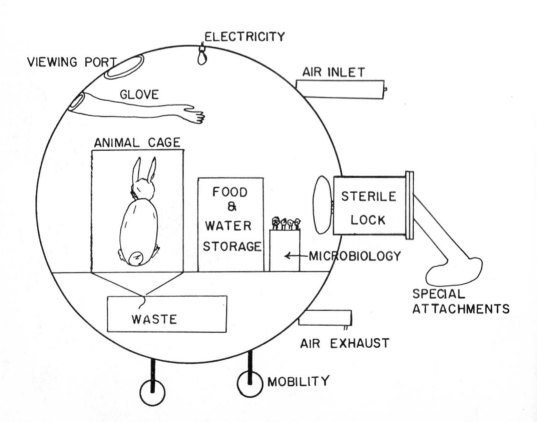

swells up enormously and prevents them from developing and living normally. The same problem had been met and successfully solved in other germfree animals. So the researchers at first tried the techniques that had worked before: limiting the amount of food that young animals were permitted to eat and limiting the amount of fiber (mainly from vegetable foods) in their diet. But these approaches were no help at all in raising germfree rabbits. The only way researchers were finally able to raise healthy germfree rabbits was to operate on them and tie off part of the caecum, so that it could not become so enlarged. With this operation, rabbits have been able to live normal

A technician hand feeds a germfree baby rabbit in a plastic film isolator.

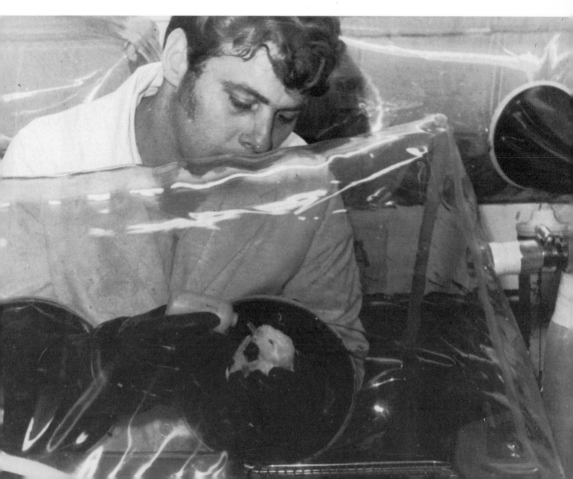

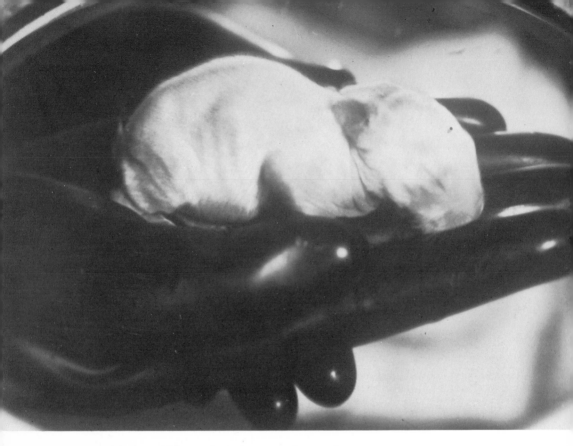

This baby rabbit was born in a germfree tank.

lives in germfree chambers, to mate, and to raise young of their own.

The difficulties that scientists met in raising germfree rabbits were not completely unexpected, for rabbits depend on the bacteria that normally live in their intestines not only for vitamins, but also to help digest the cellulose in the grasses and other foods they eat. Indeed, germfree rabbits must be given special vitamin supplements in their diet, and they are fed foods low in cellulose and much higher in starches and sugars than rabbits eat in the germ-filled world.

Now that colonies of germfree rabbits have been successfully raised, these animals, together with others, are helping scientists to study the causes of diseases and to develop effective new methods of treating them.

This rabbit has grown up without ever coming in contact with germs.

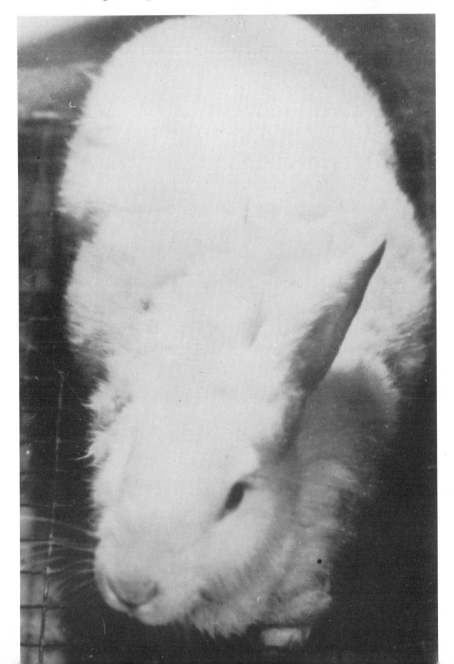

The Rabbit Family

What is the difference between a rabbit and a hare? Most people do not know. Indeed, the common names of many lagomorphs are actually wrong. The Belgian hare is a rabbit, while the jackrabbit and the snowshoe rabbit are really hares.

There are several main differences between rabbits and hares. Hares are generally larger than rabbits, with long, lanky bodies and legs, and longer ears. (The Belgian hare gets its name because it looks more like a hare than a rabbit.)

Rabbits dig burrows in the ground. Hares do not burrow. They lie out in the open in small depressions, called "forms," molded to the shape of their bodies.

Rabbit babies are born blind, deaf, naked, and helpless. Newborn hares have developed a little longer in their

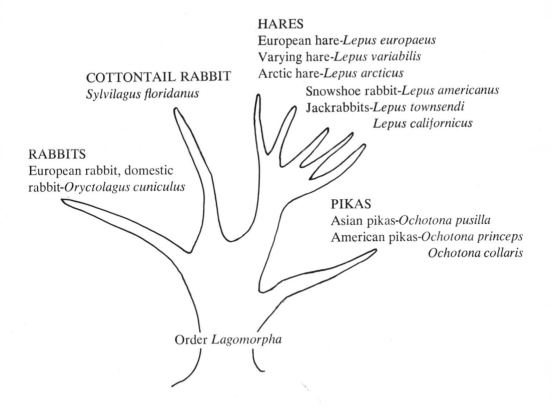

HARES
European hare-*Lepus europaeus*
Varying hare-*Lepus variabilis*
Arctic hare-*Lepus arcticus*

COTTONTAIL RABBIT
Sylvilagus floridanus

Snowshoe rabbit-*Lepus americanus*
Jackrabbits-*Lepus townsendi*
Lepus californicus

RABBITS
European rabbit, domestic
rabbit-*Oryctolagus cuniculus*

PIKAS
Asian pikas-*Ochotona pusilla*
American pikas-*Ochotona princeps*
Ochotona collaris

Order *Lagomorpha*

The Lagomorph Family Tree.

mother's body and have a full coat of fur. Their eyes and ears are open, and they can hop about within minutes after they are born.

There is a great deal of confusion in America about which are rabbits and which are hares. In the United States, anything that has long ears and hops is usually called a rabbit. The most common American rabbit, the cottontail, adds to the confusion. In some ways it is like a rabbit, and in others it resembles a hare. Cottontails are like a middle branch on the lagomorph family tree.

91

Rabbits

The rabbits that are raised all over the world as pets and food animals are descendants of the European rabbits. These animals came originally from the Mediterranean region, in southwestern Europe and northwest Africa. Humans have helped them to spread to England, Australia, and many other countries.

Today's domestic rabbits are descended from the European rabbit.

Wild rabbits are about 15 to 18 inches long, with a soft, grayish-brown fur coat that helps to camouflage them among the grass and leaves. They live in grasslands and open parts of woodlands. There they dig a maze of underground burrows, which crisscross and connect into a complicated community dwelling-place, or warren.

Wild rabbits are active mainly at night, coming out of their burrows in the late afternoon to graze in the nearby area. They return to their underground homes at sunrise to doze or rest, preen their fur, and snuggle together companionably in family groups. They keep their burrows clean, never fouling them. They urinate only when they are outdoors, and they form two sorts of droppings, neither of which is allowed to remain and dirty the burrow. During the day, while they rest, rabbits occasionally squeeze out soft pellets, which they eat before they have a chance to drop to the floor of the burrow. The food and vitamins in these pellets thus have another chance to be digested. Later, while the rabbits are out grazing, they pass small, hard pellets of waste materials, which they do not reingest. They never drop these pellets while they are inside the warren.

The way of life of wild rabbits has been very closely studied in England and in Australia, with observations over large fenced-in areas under a wide variety of natural conditions. It has even been possible to observe rabbits underground through an ingenious experimental setup: a special warren was dug and roofed over with glass, and observed from above in a room lit only by red light. The

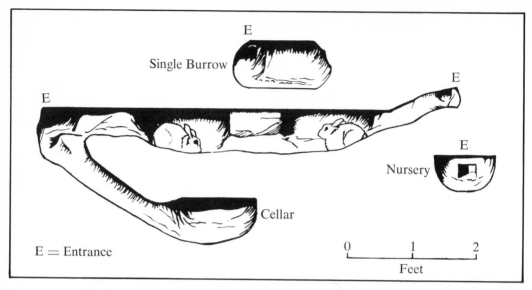

E

Single Burrow

E

E

E

Nursery

Cellar

E = Entrance

0   1   2

Feet

Scientists have observed wild rabbits in an artificial underground warren.

rabbits soon became accustomed to the red light and acted as though they were in the normal darkness of the burrow.

In the center of the warren, in the largest, driest chamber, live the king and queen and their children. The king is the strongest, most vigorous buck in the area, and the queen is his chosen mate. (He also mates with several other does, who live with their families in other rooms in the warren, outside the royal chamber.) The king does not inherit his position, although the children of the royal family, brought up under the best of conditions, are often strongest and healthiest, with the best chance of becoming king in turn. The king buck must fight to win his position and then defend it against all challengers. If he falters, a stronger challenger may win the kingship—and perhaps the queen and harem as well. The dominant buck stakes

94

out a territory in the choicest part of the area. He marks out the boundaries by "chinning": with special scent glands under his chin, he leaves his mark on the ground, plant stems, and other objects along the frontier. Other males in the king's territory must either submit to him or leave. If they acknowledge his leadership, they will be permitted to live peacefully in his land, mate, and father families of their own. If a subordinate buck leaves, he may establish a territory of his own in a nearby area.

All the furious fighting and defense of home territories take place only during the breeding season, which lasts from autumn to early summer. But then, during the late summer, a curious thing happens. The rabbits begin to molt, losing their heavy fur, and the testes (sex organs) of the males shrink and disappear up into their body cavity. Now they suddenly become friendly and sociable. Bitter rivals may be found hopping about together or dozing peacefully side-by-side in the warren. After the quiet summer off-season, rivalries begin again, and there may be some changing of partners and even the establishment of a new king.

The young "kittens" are born about four weeks after mating. Shortly before she is due to give birth, the doe digs a special burrow, away from the main tunnels of the warren. (The queen doe and some other members of the royal family may dig out rooms branching off from the royal quarters.) She lines her nest with soft grasses, and then with fur that she plucks from her own belly.

Usually there are four to six in the litter. The newborn

kittens can crawl, but they are naked and their eyes are tightly sealed shut. Their mother feeds them with her milk and then leaves the nest burrow, sealing it tightly with a stopper of packed-down earth. She will visit the nest burrow to nurse her babies only at night, and usually only once each twenty-four hours. She carefully covers the entrance again when she leaves, hiding her nest from predators.

The baby rabbits grow quickly. After about ten days, they have a coat of fur, and their eyes are open. Their ears are getting longer; when they were born their ears were so short that they hardly looked like rabbit ears at all. Their mother keeps their nest clean and dry, even licking away their droppings.

As the kittens grow larger and more active, they begin to push against the earth plug at the entrance to the nest burrow. Soon they are peeking shyly out at the world aboveground. By three weeks or so, the young rabbits

Two young rabbits sun themselves near the entrance to their burrow.

A sunny spot to take a bath.

begin to come out to nibble timidly at the grass. Their
mother no longer tries to plug up the entrance to the burrow. She watches closely for danger and warns her babies
by thumping on the ground with her hind feet and raising
her white tail like a signal flag. Her little ones copy her
actions like little mimics and scamper down into their hole.

When the young rabbits are about four weeks old, they are ready to be on their own. Their mother has most likely mated within a day or two after they were born, and now she is due to have a new litter. She digs out a new nest chamber and starts again. She may continue to have a new litter each month, all through the breeding season.

Depending on weather conditions, a young doe will be ready to breed for the first time between five or six months old and a year. The young bucks are not able to mate until they are nine or ten months old, even in mild climates.

Although the buck fights to defend his mates and his territory, it is the doe who determines where the family will live. She chooses the site for the first nest burrow, and as the group grows, the does do the heavy digging to enlarge the warren. The buck may scratch a bit to make his quarters more comfortable, but he usually gives up after a few minutes. Rabbits dig by loosening the earth with their forepaws, then kicking it backward with their hind feet.

Wild rabbits provide food for a number of meat-eaters. Aboveground, they are hunted by foxes and dogs, wild cats, domestic cats, and badgers. The rabbit has two effective lines of defense. His dull-colored coat provides camouflage that makes him hard to spot as long as he freezes, or remains absolutely still. If he is discovered by a predator anr realizes it in time, he bounds away swiftly, twisting and dodging until he can duck into a handy hole or other cover.

Three keen senses help rabbits to detect the presence of enemies. Their large, wide-spaced eyes permit them to

98

see what is happening in front and on both sides without turning their heads. Their long ears are splendid sound funnels that work like antennas to bring in the slightest sounds of danger. And the rabbits' constantly wiggling noses expose the sensitive scent detectors in their nostrils.

Like her wild ancestors, this domestic rabbit sniffs the air to find out what is going on.

Foxes, dogs, and cats generally catch rabbits only when they take them by surprise, and badgers are too slow to catch any but the young kittens. Hawks, owls, and other birds of prey are too small to carry off any but the young rabbits. Far more dangerous enemies are weasels, such as stoats and ferrets. They pursue rabbits right into their burrows and trail them by scent through the maze of the warren. Indeed, in some regions of Europe, trained ferrets are sent down into rabbit warrens to hunt rabbits for their masters. A cornered rabbit may make a stand and put up a good fight for his life. He uses his slashing teeth and, even more effectively, powerful kicks with his big hind feet, which are equipped with sharp claws. A mother doe, in particular, will fight valiantly to protect her young, defending them against cats and even weasels.

In the wild, rabbits are usually at the height of their health and strength at about twenty months of age, and few survive as long as five years. In captivity, protected from predators and disease, wild rabbits can live for ten years or more—as long as, or longer than, domesticated rabbits.

European Hares

European hares really deserve the name of lagomorph. The brown hare, found throughout cental and southern Europe, has large, heavy hind legs and long, sensitive ears. He has the typical lagomorph teeth, and his big front teeth can be seen through his deeply slotted harelip. He is about 2 feet

The European hare.

long, and his body is covered with thick, soft grayish-brown or reddish fur.

The hare's fur coat is actually two coats in one. Close to his skin there is a dense, white, woolly underfur, which keeps him warm like a suit of winter underwear. On his belly this underfur may be up to 1½ inches long. Growing out beyond the underfur is a coat of guard hairs, which give the hare his color. Each of the guard hairs is black at the tip, brownish in the middle part, and black in the part closest to the hare's body. These two fur coats help to keep the hare's body warm and dry as he lies out in the fields in all kinds of weather. Hares do not dig burrows to take shelter in. They lie out in the fields unprotected, in small depressions in the grass called forms, bcause they are hollowed out to the shape of the hare's body.

European hares are active mainly at dawn and dusk. They hop about busily, nibbling at the grass, clover, and other plants of the fields or meadows in which they live. From time to time a hare will stop and rise up on his haunches or even stand up on his hind legs to get a better look around. Nose quivering and long ears standing straight up, he scans the field for danger with his large bright eyes.

During the day, hares rest in their forms. It might seem as though the hare is quite defenseless as he lies out in the open field. Foxes, lynxes, and weasels could easily pounce on him, and hawks and owls could swoop down from the sky to seize him in their talons. But the hare has two excellent defenses. First, he is nearly invisible. His brownish coat blends with the soil and grasses and provides a near-perfect camouflage. Unless he moves, one would never know he was there. And he does not move. He knows how to keep perfectly still to make the most of his camouflage.

Though the hare may rest, he is alert for signs of danger. His nostrils twitch continuously, testing the air for suspicious scents. His keen ears can pick up a telltale rustle of leaves or crackling of twigs. If danger approaches, he is suddenly up and away in a tawny flash. Bounding along with thrusts of his heavy hind legs, the hare can run more than 40 miles an hour. He is so fast that even a racing greyhound cannot begin to overtake him until the hare starts to tire. But the hare does not run straight ahead. Instead, he zigs and zags erratically, takes soaring 15 foot leaps to clear a hedge or a wall, doubles back on his own tracks, and does not hesitate to take to the water, swimming strongly to escape his pursuer. Often a dog may follow a hare's scent, only to stop in puzzlement as the trail mysteriously seems to come to a dead end.

Hares are normally not very sociable animals. They prefer to live alone. But when it is mating time, they seek out the company of other hares. Mating can occur at any time of the year, but it reaches a peak in the early spring, around March. The old saying, "mad as a March hare," comes from the strange behavior of the male hares (jacks) in March. During the spring mating season, jacks can often be found locked in fierce battles. The fight begins with a sparring match. The two jacks rear up on their hind legs and hit out at each other with their forepaws like

Two "March hares" box furiously . . .

boxers in a ring. Soon the fight may progress to biting and kicking. Powerful hind legs can do real damage as they kick at each other's bellies or leap over each other, getting in a kick on the way. Usually one hare decides he has had enough and breaks away to run off. Often the victor follows him for a distance to make sure he has learned his lesson.

Curiously, during the mad March season, jacks may also be found fighting with does (females). If the doe is not in the mood for mating, the fight may be in earnest—and since she is a bit larger than her would-be mate, she can generally make her point. But if the doe is ready for mating, her boxing session seems more playful and may soon give way to nuzzling and licking.

The litter, usually between two and four babies, is born about forty-two days after mating. Young hares, called "leverets," are born in a grass-lined nest in the open field. They are open-eyed and alert, with a full coat of fur. They can move about actively almost immediately, and they quickly scatter. Each makes its own small form, and there it rests. The mother hare visits each of her brood in the morning and again in the evening, to feed them with her milk. This is the most dangerous age for hares. The only defense the young leverets have is to freeze to use their camouflage to the best advantage. Many of them are killed by weasels or mink, foxes or wildcats, hawks, or owls.

until one gives up and runs away.

Their scattering, each to his own form, helps to increase the chances that at least some of the litter will survive.

The young hares grow quickly. They begin to nibble grass and other low-growing plants, and after two weeks they are ready to be weaned. In another few weeks they are ready to live independently of their mother (who very likely is now ready to have another litter). At eight months—if they have survived that long—they are old enough to mate, and they reach their full adult size at about a year.

Hares are hunted by many natural enemies. The furred and feathered meat-eaters of the wilds normally help to keep hares from multiplying so fast that they overrun the fields. But the most dangerous enemy of the hares is man. Not only do humans trap them and hunt them with dogs, but they also kill them without meaning to. Many hares, particularly the defenseless leverets, are killed by farm machinery and by pesticides sprayed on the fields.

In the parts of Europe where brown hares live, the winters are generally rather mild. But in northern Europe, snow covers the ground through most of the winter months. Brown fur would stand out sharply against the white snow, and the camouflage would be lost. The Alpine hares of northern Europe have adapted to the changing seasons by changing their coats twice a year. As the days grow shorter in the autumn, the brown hairs in the coats of the Alpine hares begin to fall out and are replaced by white hairs. At this time the hares' coats are a mixture of brown and white hairs and look blue. As a result, another common name for these hares is "blue hares." (They are also called European varying hares because they change their color with the seasons.) By the time the snows of winter have fallen, the Alpine hare's coat is pure white except for the black fur on the tips of his ears. Then in the spring, as the days grow longer again, he gradually sheds his white fur for a new coat of brown.

A number of other kinds of hares, very much like the European hares, are found in Asia, Africa, and America.

American Hares

The largest of all the hares live far up in the frozen North, at the top of the North American continent and in Greenland. These Arctic hares may grow up to 30 inches long and weigh up to 15 pounds.

In some of the Arctic regions, it is winter nearly all year round. Cold winds whistle along the snow-covered ground; the ground is bare for only a few weeks or months of brief summer. But the Arctic hares are especially well adapted to survive under these harsh conditions. Their fur is soft, thick, and fine, and covers their whole bodies—even the soles of their feet. The Arctic hares that live farthest north have a pure-white coat all year long. Crouching in the snow, with their black-tipped ears laid back, they are quite invisible. Their relatives who live farther south, in Alaska and Newfoundland, change their white winter coat for a brown summer coat, which they wear for only a few months. If winter snows are late, the Arctic hares are out of luck. Their white winter coats stand out sharply against the bare ground, and Eskimos find them easy hunting.

The Arctic hare in his white winter coat.

What can these big hares find to eat in the barren lands of the Arctic? They feed mainly on willow leaves, buds, bark, twigs, and roots. In the summer they also eat grasses and leaves and flowers of other plants. In winter their keen sense of smell tells them where a tasty willow twig or other bit of food is buried. An Arctic hare, hopping along, may stop suddenly, as if he were drawn by a magnet, and immediately start to dig down into the snow. He may have to break through a hard crust of snow with his front paws first, and then dig down a foot or two to reach his prize. His four front teeth are particularly large and stick out like pairs of tweezers. He uses them to pluck out bits of food from under the snow, and also to scrape off lichens from the windswept rocks.

Arctic hares are sociable, and usually stay together in herds of up to a hundred. But in the spring, mating time, the males become short-tempered. They rear up on their hind legs and box with each other or slash viciously with their teeth.

After about two weeks, the mating season is over and the herds break up. Alone or in pairs, the hares move out over the tundra. About a month later, in late May or June, the litters are born. The young hares, usually about five to seven in a litter, have a woolly coat of fur, the same color as their parents'. Their eyes are open, but they are helpless and stay in the nest. They huddle together for warmth, for their mother comes to the nest only to feed them. If danger comes near, they freeze, crouching down with their eyes closed and their ears flattened back. When they are half grown, they begin to run from enemies, dodging to try to escape.

Arctic hares are an important link in the chain of life in the Arctic. They feed on plants and turn them into animal protein. They are fed upon, in turn, by foxes, wolves, snowy owls, and other hunters of the North. The Eskimos, too, prize Arctic hares, not only as a source of food, but also for their soft fur, which makes warm socks, mittens, and blankets.

Farther south, in Canada and the northern United States, live the snowshoe rabbits. These animals are really hares, not rabbits. They get their name from their big feet, with wide-spread toes and soles covered with long, coarse fur. The snowshoe rabbit's "snowshoes" help him to move easily through all but the deepest snows.

The snowshoe rabbit gets his name from his big feet.

This hare is also called the varying hare. Like the European varying hare and some of the Arctic hares, snowshoe rabbits change their coat twice a year. Late in autumn, the brown summer coat begins to change to the white coat of winter. The new white winter hairs actually begin to grow in before the old hairs are lost, so the varying hare is kept warm even while he is shedding his summer fur. In the spring his color changes in a similar way to brown again. The change is gradual, starting at the ears and feet and taking about ten weeks to complete.

Scientists have wondered what makes snowshoe rabbits and other varying hares change color with the seasons. Their summer and winter coats are excellent adaptations to the changing lands where they live, brown earth in summer and white snow in winter. Their fur usually matches their surroundings and helps to camouflage and protect them from the keen eyes of their enemies. But they cannot change their color to match their surroundings exactly, as some fish and other animals do. If the snows are late, the hares may already have changed into their winter coats—and then their white fur works against them. It is not temperature that triggers the change, either, for if a varying hare is kept indoors in a heated room, it will still change to a white winter coat in the autumn. It is as though it has an inner calendar that follows the seasons of the year.

Experiments have shown that this inner calendar is governed by the length of the days. In the winter, days are short and nights are long. As spring approaches, days grow longer; they reach their longest point in midsummer, and

White fur provides good camouflage in the snow.

then grow shorter again. A varying hare kept in a laboratory under artificial light can be made to change the color of its coat by changing the number of hours of artificial daylight, no matter what the temperature. If the days are shortened, its coat will turn white even in a warm room. On the other hand, eighteen hours of artificial light each day will change a white coat to brown or prevent a brown coat from changing to white when the temperature is winter cold.

The snowshoe rabbit takes good care of his fur coat. Often he takes a dust bath in a warm sunny spot. Then he scratches all over, and combs out his fur with the claws of his hind feet. Like a housecat, he washes his face with his forepaws, then licks his paws and his hind legs thoroughly, one at a time.

The snowshoe rabbit is a forest animal. He especially likes to stay in thickets of underbrush, where he can hide from his enemies. He is hunted by foxes, weasels, and birds of prey. When his camouflage fails him, he falls back on his second line of defense—his strong hind legs. This hare can go from a relaxed sitting position to a full-speed leaping run almost instantly. Sailing along, he may cover 12 feet in each bound. Dodging and twisting, he often leaves a pursuing dog or fox hopelessly confused.

The snowshoe rabbit runs fast—up to 30 miles an hour —but he does not usually run far. Before long he begins to circle, and soon he is back, close to his starting point again. A shrewd hunter whose dog has flushed a snowshoe rabbit needs only to wait, and he will likely have another shot at

The snowshoe rabbit is a forest animal.

the rabbit on its way back. One Wisconsin biologist followed a snowshoe rabbit for more than an hour. Frightened as it was, the fleeing hare did not go outside its home territory of about ten acres. If hares are trapped and then released in woods outside their home range, they usually try to return to their old home. Up to about a mile, they can generally find their way. But in one experiment of this kind, no hares released three miles from home were able to return successfully.

During the day, the snowshoe rabbit, like his European relatives, rests in a form on the ground. He may have several forms scattered around his home territory, but his favorite is usually on a slight rise in the ground, where he has the best view of approaching enemies and is sheltered by overhanging branches or bushes. He goes out to feed mainly at dusk and at dawn, following hard-packed trails that he has made in the leaves and debris of the forest floor.

In the summer, snowshoe rabbits feed mainly on grasses, clover, dandelions, and other herbs, as well as tender buds and shoots of bushes. But in the winter food is harder to find, and the hares eat bark and twigs of trees. They often eat the bark in a ring all the way around a slender tree trunk. A tree that is girdled in this way will die, for it cannot transport its nutrients from one part to another across the gap of missing bark. In the forest this girdling of young trees does not do much harm and may even be helpful, keeping the trees from crowding each other too much. But when hungry hares get into orchards or plantings of valuable lumber trees, they can cause expensive damage.

Snowshoe rabbits are not very sociable, preferring to remain alone most of the time. They do not chase away other hares that happen to wander near, however, and sometimes a group will gather in a clearing on a moonlit night and sit quietly together. Occasionally the forest resounds with a strange thumping, as a snowshoe rabbit drums on the ground with his hind feet to warn other hares of danger. In the spring, the males may sometimes quarrel, but they do not usually fight for a mate. A male chases a female through the forest, the two of them leaping and dodging. When she is ready to mate, she stops and lets him catch her.

About thirty-six days after mating, the litter is born. The mother snowshoe rabbit does not build a nest, but simply has her babies on the ground wherever she happens to be. There are usually three or four young, but there may be up to ten. The babies nurse for the first time right after they are born, but after that their mother feeds them only at night. She usually remains close by and may bravely fight to defend them from a weasel or other predator.

The newborn leverets are covered with fine, thick, brown fur, and they can walk and hop almost immediately. They grow quickly, and in less than two weeks they are nibbling on grass and other tender plants. Their mother weans them when they are about four weeks old. They are old enough to mate at about a year. Although snowshoe rabbits can live up to about eight years, most die much earlier of disease or are caught by predators.

Another type of American rabbit that is really a hare is

Three young snowshoe rabbits found by a hunting dog in Redvers, Saskatchewan.

the jackrabbit. This hare, common in the western United States, gets his name from his long "jackass" ears and long-legged, lanky appearance. A 24-inch-long antelope jackrabbit, for instance, has ears more than 8 inches long. These superantennas stand straight up and turn back and forth to catch sounds of possible danger. When the jackrabbit races along, at up to 45 miles an hour, he lays his long ears back flat against his shoulders.

When the jackrabbit is not in such a hurry, he has a

The California jackrabbit.

habit of bounding along with an extra-high jump each four or five. During this high jump, clear of the tops of the grasses or brush, he looks around to see whether there is any danger. His keen eyes, ears, and nose are a good early-warning system. The antelope jackrabbit has an even odder habit. If he is fleeing from an enemy, he dodges back and forth, exposing a patch of white fur on his rump. The white signal is always on the side pointing toward the danger and is believed to be a warning signal for other rabbits.

The jackrabbit's main enemy is the coyote. Coyotes cannot run as fast as jackrabbits, so they must often use their wits to catch their prey. A coyote may sneak up on a jackrabbit when he is sleeping; or it may try to outguess the fleeing hare and cut across to intercept him when he circles back. Often coyotes hunt in pairs, with one chasing and the other waiting to see which way the jackrabbit will run. The jackrabbit has some tricks of his own. He knows every inch of his territory, and zigs and zags to take advantage of every bit of cover and underbrush that might hamper a pursuing enemy. (Jackrabbits usually live in open plains areas, where they can use their speed and tremendous leaps to good advantage.) Another favorite trick is to duck unexpectedly under a barbed-wire fence, leaving the pursuer to run into it.

Often the jackrabbit does not need to use his speed to remain safe from enemies. His light-brown, salt-and-pepper coat provides good camouflage when he is resting quietly in his form with his long legs folded under him. Some white-tailed jackrabbits that live farther north change to a white coat in the winter, when the ground is covered with snow.

Jackrabbits living in hot, dry regions usually rest during the heat of the day. They go out to forage in the late afternoon and nibble almost continuously at grasses and other succulent plants until the early morning hours. They do not need to drink much water; they get the moisture they need from the plants they eat. During the driest months, they may eat cactus, such as the prickly pear. When a jackrabbit eats a particularly spiny variety of cactus, such as the cholla, he first bites around a patch of spines and

A white-tailed jackrabbit in his winter coat.

pulls it away. Then he carefully pokes his nose into the opening he has made and munches on the pulp. When food is scarce in the jackrabbits' home territory, bands of them may invade farmers' fields of alfalfa or other crops. In addition to eating a geat deal (fifteen antelope jackrabbits can eat as much as a sheep), they cut down and waste much grass, and spoil good foraging lands when they are too numerous.

Sometimes, on moonlit nights, groups of jackrabbits can be seen gathered together in a strange sort of dance. They form a circle and move inward toward the center. Then suddenly they leap into the air and scatter. Soon they repeat the movement.

The mating season starts in the early spring and goes on into the summer. Fights among male jackrabbits are frequent. They stand up on their hind legs and box with their forefeet. Whenever there is an opportunity, the jack gets in a vicious kick with a hind foot. His strong claws may rip the other jack severely.

About six weeks after mating, the mother jackrabbit digs out an oval depression in the ground in some sheltered spot. She lines the nest with fur that she pulls out of her own coat, and there she has her litter. Black-tailed jackrabbits usually have only one to three young, but white-tailed jackrabbits have an average of four. Their mother feeds them, then covers them with a blanket of fine grass or fur. She stays in a form where she can keep an eye on the nest—but not close enough to risk leading a predator to her babies. Unless she must rush to their defense, she

121

usually visits them only in the dark of night. Within a few days the baby jackrabbits are nibbling at grasses, and in a few weeks or less they are on their own.

Cottontail Rabbits

Cottontail rabbits are the exception to the rule of how to tell a rabbit from a hare. These small furry mammals are found all over the United States and Mexico, and down to the northern part of South America. They do not burrow, as European rabbits do, but live on the surface in thick underbrush and thickets of briers. Yet they are not like the hares, for their babies are born blind, naked, and helpless. Cottontail rabbits' ears are much shorter than hares' ears, too.

A cottontail rabbit crouches in the tall grass.

Cottontail rabbits are small animals, about 15 inches long. They have a peppered brown fur coat, white on the belly and legs, with a fluffy white cottontail that is held up like a white signal flag. Like the other lagomorphs, they have large eyes and keen ears and noses to warn them of danger. When an enemy threatens, a cottontail may freeze until the last possible moment, taking advantage of its camouflage, before turning suddenly into a bounding, dodging blur of brown fur. (We once accidentally stepped on a young cottontail crouching in the field behind our house. A frightened squeak made us look down, but when we parted the grass and bent down to look at it, it catapulted away.) As soon as it can, the fleeing cottontail takes refuge in a bramble patch or old abandoned hole dug by a fox or badger. It knows every foot of its home territory, which is crisscrossed by rabbit trails and marked by scent signposts that the rabbit leaves with the scent glands under its chin.

Cottontail rabbits generally prefer the borderland between woods and fields, where there is plenty of cover. They feed on all kinds of vegetation—grasses, clover, buds, twigs and bark, and vegetables in fields and gardens. They are most active in the twilight hours, but they can be seen about at any hour of the day. During the spring and summer mating season, we have often seen them hopping about in twos, chasing one another and engaging in a sort of leaping mating dance.

The father cottontail does not stay with his mate very long. She usually turns on him a few days after mating and

The New England cottontail.

chases him out of her territory with vicious bites. Her litter, an average of four or five young, will be born about a month after mating. Before it arrives, she scoops out a round depression in the ground—in a sheltered spot or even in an open field—and lines it with grasses and fur that she plucks from her belly. If she happens to be far from the nest when her babies are born, she carries each one in her mouth to place him in the nest. Then she covers the litter with a felted blanket of grass and bits of fur, scatters some leaves over it, and goes to rest a short distance away, where she can watch without attracting predators to the nest. In the dark of night, she returns to feed her young; when they are full, she covers them and leaves them again.

By the time the young cottontails are about a week old, they have a full coat of fur, and their eyes and ears open. They begin to squeak and hop about. Their mother keeps watch and will quickly answer a cry for help. She will bravely attack a cat or dog or snake that threatens her young.

At about twelve days, the young rabbits begin to spend some time outside the nest. They nibble at plants and rest in small forms nearby. In a few more days they leave the nest entirely. For a while they feed and frolic near their mother. She seems to like their company, although she is soon busy raising her next litter. Gradually the young ones wander farther away to find territories of their own. They are mature enough to mate at about six months, but do not usually have young of their own until the following spring.

Cottontail rabbits can live for two or three years, but studies have shown that few of them even reach their first birthday. Many of the young are killed by the cold or wet while they are still in the nest. Others fall victim to lawnmowers or farmers' machines and sprays. Both young and adult cottontails are prey for practically all the meat-eat-

125

ers, from hawks and owls to foxes, weasels, dogs, cats, and snakes. Even squirrels and crows may attack young rabbits. The snows of winter take a heavy toll. Unlike snowshoe rabbits, cottontails have a hard time getting around in the snow, and their floundering makes them easy prey for foxes and other predators. When it snows, they usually huddle in their sheltered forms and do not even try to feed.

A cottontail rabbit stands up to look around.

Cottontails, like other lagomorphs, may also be killed by various diseases. The most serious of these is "tularemia," or rabbit fever. This disease is spread by lice, ticks, and fleas. Humans can catch it by handling or eating sick rabbits. It is a wise rule never to touch a cottontail (or any other wild animal) that acts sick or is slow-moving, and rabbit meat should be cooked thoroughly before it is eaten.

Humans kill countless numbers of cottontail rabbits each year, either unintentionally with automobiles and farm machinery, or on purpose because they can be serious pests to farm crops. Yet humans also unintentionally help cottontails survive by killing foxes, coyotes, hawks, and other predators that would otherwise help to keep their numbers in check.

Cats and dogs sometimes find a cottontail nest and bring the young rabbits home. The best thing to do with them is to put them back. Although the mother cottontail will abandon a nest that has been disturbed before she has had her litter, she does not seem to be as bothered by a disturbance after her babies are born. (She may move them to a new nest if she thinks they are in danger.) But if you can't find the nest, it is a great temptation to try to raise the tiny cottontails. If you decide to do so, be prepared for hard work and possible disappointment. You will need to feed the babies every hour or so at first. You can use a baby formula, diluted half and half with water, and feed it with a medicine dropper or a doll's baby bottle. The little orphans should be kept in a warm, dry box with a soft nest of rags or wood shavings. As they get stronger, you can give them strained baby vegetables, and later shredded lettuce and raw carrots. As soon as they are old enough to get about and feed by themselves, you should release them in some suitable place outdoors. (In many states it is illegal to keep wild animals as pets.)

The Pika

Since the name Lagomorph comes from words meaning "hare-shaped," there is one member of the group that does not really seem to belong. This is the pika. It is not hare-shaped at all: its ears are rounded, not long, its hind legs are about the same length as its forelegs, and its tiny tail is hidden in fur. It looks rather like a fat, furry guinea pig. But the pika does have the typical lagomorph teeth, with six incisors in front. And many of its habits are very similar to those of its cousins, the rabbits and hares.

Pikas live mainly in cold, barren lands in the mountains of the northwestern United States and Canada, in the Russian steppes, and in other regions of northern Asia and eastern Europe. Most pikas make their homes in piles of loose rocks heaped up by rockslides. They scamper sure-footedly over the treacherous rocks, gripping them firmly with their tiny hair-soled feet.

A rock pile might seem like a grim, unfriendly place to live, but for pikas it provides a safe haven. A strange noise or the shadow of a passing eagle or hawk sends them popping down into convenient cracks and crevices in the

A pika on a rocky perch.

rocks, squeaking a high-pitched warning cry as they disappear. Only weasels and martens can follow them into
their rocky refuges, and even these predators may get lost
in the winding tunnels.

Pikas are sociable little creatures and are often found
living together in large groups. But each pika has a small
area that is all his own. There among the rocks are his
burrow and storerooms, as well as favorite resting places
where he basks in the sun. And not too far from the rock-
pile are the fields where the pika gathers his food.

The pika's day begins at dawn. As soon as the sun is up, the little "rock rabbit" is up and about, making the rounds of his territory. He scampers nimbly from one favorite spot to another. At each he pauses to look around. Eyes darting, nose twitching, and two round ears spread like twin antennas, he scans the area for danger. From time to time he sends out the high-pitched calls that have won pikas the name of "whistling hares." The mountainside echoes with the squeaks of dozens of pikas as they call back and forth to each other. It might seem dangerous for a small defenseless animal to be so noisy. But the pika is a skilled ventriloquist—his cries often seem to be coming from anywhere but where he really is.

When the pika has finished his rounds, he heads out to he fields to collect his dinner. Like the other lagomorphs, the pika is a vegetarian. He eats grasses and leaves, fruits and berries. Sometimes he may even climb a small tree to nibble the young shoots. In areas where vegetation is scarce, pikas will gather almost anything that is green, even moss and lichens. But in regions with lush plant life, they are more choosy, harvesting only the kinds of plants they particularly like.

The trips to and from the fields are the most dangerous times for the pika. Out there he has no convenient cracks in the rocks to disappear into if a hawk or eagle swoops down. So he does not linger. With his sharp, chisellike teeth, he snips off plant stems or tugs at small plants to pull them up by the roots. He gathers exactly as much as he can carry crosswise in his jaws, and then he trots home again.

130

When the midday sun is high in the sky, it is time for a siesta. If it is not too hot, the pikas lie on flat rocks and bask in the sun. Even in mid-winter, when the temperature is below zero, pikas will often scamper across patches of snow to lie in the sun on a rock that the wind has swept bare. But if the temperature is above 90° F or so, they retire to the coolness of the caverns below. Then in the afternoon they are back to work again, until the sun sets.

Summers are short in the northern lands where pikas live, and the winters are very cold. But pikas do not hibernate. And somehow, as the late summer days grow shorter, these small creatures know that they must lay up a store of food. Carefully the pika places the grasses and other plants he has gathered on a flat rock to dry and cure in the

A pika carrying hay.

sun. The next day he lays a new layer on top of the one before. Often in his rounds he rests on top of his growing mound, and his small dry, pelletlike droppings can be found mixed among the drying plants. Eventually his haystack may be several feet high, containing up to fifty pounds of hay.

If a storm threatens, it is a great emergency. Whistling calls echo back and forth as groups of pikas work together, pulling and tugging at grasses and plant stems to take them underground before they can be spoiled by the rain. After the storm has passed, they bring the hay piles back up to dry in the sun again.

Pikas will work far into the night if their harvest is threatened by a storm. But usually sundown means bedtime, and they retire to their burrows to rest. During the night, a pika's droppings are different from the dry daytime pellets. The night pellets are black and wrapped in a jellylike layer that keeps them moist. Like the rabbits and hares, the pika does a strange thing: he swallows his nighttime droppings. They remain in his stomach until morning, when they will be mixed with the fresh food he eats and then pass through his intestines to be digested again. The nighttime droppings are rich in vitamins, produced by bacteria that live in the pika's intestines. If he did not eat them, he would lose these valuable nutrients.

As winter approaches, the pikas drag their hay down into cracks in the rocks and store it there, protected from the snow. During the coldest months, the pikas spend most of their time in their burrows, conserving energy by resting. They come out only to feed, and sometimes to bask in a patch of winter sunshine. Their unusually soft, fluffy fur keeps them warm in even the coldest weather. Most pikas have gray or buffy gray fur. But some change their coats twice a year, with reddish fur in the summer and a gray coat in the winter.

In April, when spring comes, it is mating time for the pikas. A month after mating, the mother pika gives birth to from three to five tiny naked, helpless babies. In a grass-lined nest, deep in her burrow, she feeds them with her milk for about two weeks. Then they are old enough to be weaned and begin to gather their own food, although they stay near their mother for some time more. A young pika grows to his adult size in just six or seven weeks. He will live for up to three years.

After the first litter is weaned, the mother pika is ready to mate again. She may have three litters during the sum-mer, the last in September.

Pikas are harmless little creatures that do not bother man's crops. They are not usually hunted for fur or food because they generally live in mountainous places that are difficult to reach, and they are so timid that they are hard to spot and catch. In fact, the first pikas were not discov-ered until 1769, in Asia, and the pikas in North America were not described until more than half a century later.

Man has found some uses for pikas. Russian farmers and sable hunters sometimes hunt for pikas' haystacks and use them for fodder for their animals. And recently scien-tists in the U.S.S.R. have begun to use pikas as laboratory animals. They are as gentle and easy to raise as guinea pigs.

The World of the Rabbit

Nose to the ground, a dog trots busily across the field. He is following a scent. He does not see the cottontail rabbit crouching motionless among the tall grasses, but he knows that the smell will lead them to something interesting. He is almost there when suddenly there is a blur of motion. The rabbit sails up, straight over the head of the startled dog, and bounds away. Barking eagerly, the dog turns to give chase. The rabbit darts and dodges, zigzagging unpredictably as the dog follows the bobbing white tail. Then suddenly the dog pulls up short and howls in dismay. The cottontail has disappeared into a thorny patch of briers. There he crouches, safe inside the maze of runways that he and other rabbits have chewed out among the thorny branches.

A cottontail rabbit on the alert.

The Balance of Nature

The world of life is divided among the eaters and the eaten. Some animals, such as field mice, rabbits, and sheep, live on grass and other plant foods. Others, from weasels to lions, must kill to fill their bellies. The killers of the animal world are called predators, and those that they kill are their prey.

A predator does not kill because he is cruel or because he enjoys making other animals suffer. He kills simply because he must in order to survive. For the prey animals of the world, one of the most important activities of each day of life is the constant struggle to avoid being eaten.

135

In a way, although it is not much consolation to the individual animals they eat, predators do a service for their prey. For they usually catch and eat mainly the weak and the sick, leaving the strongest and smartest of the prey animals to survive and reproduce their kind. If predators were too successful and wiped out the whole population of prey animals, they too would perish, for they would no longer have anything to eat.

And so, in the world of nature, a delicate balance is gradually established. The prey animals grow and reproduce, and they in turn provide food for the predators who catch them—but not all of them. As time goes on, even

Predators help to keep the world of nature in balance. This fox has just caught a cottontail.

though new individuals are continually being born and dying, the numbers of predators and prey remain about the same.

Sometimes things can upset the balance of nature. If humans kill off the predators in an area, for example, more of the prey animals will have a chance to grow to maturity and mate and raise their young. Then the mice and rabbits and other prey animals in the area will have a sudden population explosion, rapidly multiplying to far higher numbers than before. But such a population explosion does not go on forever. In time other things, such as disease or lack of food, put a limit on their numbers, and a new balance is struck.

Rabbits and hares are among the prey animals of the world. During every waking moment of every day, they must be on the alert for possible danger. They have a number of defenses, of course. Their fur provides a camouflage that makes them very hard to see, and some hares even change the color of their fur with the seasons, which gives them better protection all year round. Their great speed and unpredictable dodging saves them from the jaws of many a hungry predator. And a slashing, kicking rabbit can often be more than a match for a hunting weasel or fox.

Yet, like most prey animals, the lagomorph's best defense is a more subtle one: the ability to reproduce rapidly and in large numbers. Most rabbits and hares can bear young before they are a year old. They have many young at a time, and they often can have one litter after another,

137

The lagomorph's best defense.

only a month apart. Many of these young perish long before they are full-grown—in the jaws of weasels or foxes, coyotes or wild cats, hawks and owls and eagles, snakes, and even squirrels. Yet there are so many of them that though individuals may perish, some of their kind will survive.

Population Cycles

Studies of animal populations have revealed some curious patterns. Records of trappers, collected by the Hudson Bay Company, have yielded much information. For example, it has been found that the numbers of snowshoe rabbits vary over a cycle of about nine or ten years. Gradually the population builds up from year to year until enormous numbers are reached. In one region of Canada, it was estimated that the snowshoe rabbit population was once as high as 5,000 per square mile. Then suddenly, the population crashes. Without warning, the numbers drop to perhaps a tenth of what they were the year before.

What causes these tremendous population crashes? Could it be that more predators are eating the hares? Indeed, it has been found that lynxes, great horned owls, and goshawks have population cycles of their own, which follow the nine- or ten-year cycle of the snowshoe rabbit. As the numbers of prey build up, they can support larger and larger populations of predators. But pressure from predators is not the whole answer. The peak of the lynx population, for example, generally occurs one year *after* the peak of the snowshoe rabbits. Then the lynxes suffer their own population crash, as many of them starve to death for lack of prey.

Another factor that can help to limit an exploding lagomorph population is the food supply. Only so much grass and other plant life can grow in a particular region. As the number of animals eating it grows, eventually there may not be enough to go around. Driven by their hunger, the hares may even kill trees by girdling them, and eat the grass down to its roots, thus cutting down the supply of food for future generations.

Epidemics of diseases can sweep through large groups of animals at the peak of their population cycle, thus helping to reduce their numbers.

Scientists have found that there is still another factor that helps to limit runaway animal populations. Peculiar things begin to happen to animals when they are crowded. In snowshoe rabbits, for example, the stress of overcrowding causes changes in their livers. The liver normally stores an animal starch called glycogen. Glycogen is easily changed into glucose, the sugar that animals use for a source of energy. When snowshoe rabbits are overcrowded, their livers do not store as much glycogen as usual. The fear and excitement provoked by the approach of a predator would normally stimulate them to a leaping run. But that requires energy. So, instead, the hares with livers damaged by the stress of overcrowding may simply lie down and die before the predator has even reached them.

After the population crash, the few survivors find themselves in a world of plenty. There is abundant food, the predators are soon in balance, and gradually they build up their numbers again.

Man Interferes

The rises and falls of the snowshoe rabbit populations are natural cycles, caused and controlled by forces of nature. But when man steps in and changes the natural environment, rabbits and hares can get out of hand.

In the western United States, for example, ranchers have called for campaigns to get rid of coyotes and other predators, who sometimes prey on sheep and other livestock. Programs of trapping and poisoning have wiped out large numbers of coyotes, but some results have been unexpected. With their main enemy under control, jackrabbits have multiplied. As they become crowded, these hares begin to ruin good grazing land, eating so much grass that other, less desirable, plants move in. Bands of them may raid neighboring farms and eat the green crops. Then the farmers and ranchers must turn their attention to getting rid of the jackrabbits. Poisoned baits are scattered, and sometimes ranchers organize huge jackrabbit drives. They gather in a circle around an infested area and slowly move inward toward the center. The frightened jackrabbits dodge away from the moving men, but at first, because the circle is so large, they do not realize which way danger lies and dart in toward the center of the circle. As the circle of men tightens around them, the jackrabbits are forced into wire enclosures and killed.

In other areas where farmers try to control marauding rabbits and hares with poisons and traps, they find their efforts boomeranging in different ways. In some cases, the traps and poisons kill many of the natural predators that could have helped to keep the rabbits in check, and the farmers soon find they have more rabbits than ever. In cases where rabbit-control programs are successful, the hungry predators may grow bolder and seek the farmer's livestock to fill their bellies.

Rabbit Invasions

Yet all these problems, which have plagued man at least since the time of the ancient Romans, are mild in comparison with the troubles that result when rabbits are introduced into areas where there are few natural predators or none at all. Back in the fifteenth century, Portuguese sailors were in the habit of carrying rabbits on their ships as a ready source of fresh meat. They released some rabbits on the island of Porto Santo in 1418. There were no natural predators on the island to keep the rabbits in check. Before long, the rabbits had multiplied to the point where they ate every blade of grass and turned the island into a barren wasteland. Finally the human inhabitants of the island were forced to move, abandoning the island to the rabbit invaders.

There was a similar occurrence on Smith Island, in Washington State. Around 1900, a lighthouse keeper began raising domestic rabbits and selling their meat. Later another lighthouse keeper took over, and let all the remaining rabbits go. Before this happened, Smith Island was a bird refuge, where puffins, murres, and other sea birds nested. But the quickly multiplying rabbits stripped all the vegetation off the island. Their burrows undermined the soil, and parts of the land began caving in and slipping into the water. Soon even the rabbits were hungry and diseased because of their overcrowding. Only a massive poisoning program finally brought them under control.

In Porto Santo and Smith Island, the rabbit invaders were confined to small islands. But in Australia and New Zealand, the rabbits had a whole continent to spread over, and they took full advantage of the opportunity.

The native mammals of the Australian continent are all marsupials, animals who carry their young in pouches, and monotremes, the egg-laying mammals. Early human settlers brought dogs with them. (Some ultimately went wild and became the ancestors of today's dingos.) They also—unintentionally—brought along some rats and mice. More recent settlers introduced sheep and set up a success-

142

ful sheep-raising operation on the grassy plains. But there was nothing on the whole continent that resembled a rabbit or a hare; nor were there any natural predators that could successfully control a rabbit invasion. That invasion came in 1859. A settler from England, Thomas Austin, was lonesome for the animals of his native land. He ordered a dozen pairs of wild rabbits from England and let them free on his estate in Victoria province in Australia, intending to use them for hunting sport. Within six years, he had killed twenty thousand rabbits on his estate, and there were still thousands left! Meanwhile, the rabbits had quickly spread to neighboring estates, and onward across the countryside. Rabbit meat and fur soon became big business in Australia. But the rabbits stripped the countryside of grass, and the sheep-raising industry suffered.

Soon it was realized that the multiplying rabbits brought more losses than gains. An enormous campaign was mounted to exterminate the rabbits. Bounties were offered for rabbit tails, and millions were collected. But the rabbits

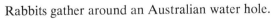

Rabbits gather around an Australian water hole.

Part of Australia's rabbit fence. Rabbits were free to roam on the left and stripped the land bare.

still kept multiplying. It was soon discovered that tailless rabbits were hopping about the countryside. They were not a new variety of rabbit—just the result of the greed of the trappers, who cut off rabbits' tails and then let them go to breed more bounties for the next year. More than a million dollars was spent to build 2,000 miles of rabbit fence across the land in a frantic effort to protect regions the rabbits had not yet reached. But that did not work either. One little hole, only a few inches across, was enough to let the rabbit hordes through into the virgin lands.

The answer finally came from South America. In 1897, all the rabbits in the hospital laboratories in Montevideo mysteriously died. It was eventually discovered that the Brazilian cottontails carry a virus disease called myxomatosis. It is a mild disease for the cottontails, spread by the bites of mosquitoes. But European rabbits have no defenses against myxomatosis. When infected mosquitoes carry the disease to them, they die.

144

Now scientists had a powerful weapon against the rabbit invaders of Australia: the myxoma virus. After a series of experiments, they introduced the virus into Australia, and it spread like wildfire. Rabbits died by the millions, and the land began to turn green again.

The battle is not yet over. In recent years there have been signs that the myxoma virus may be changing to less potent forms. And rabbits with a natural resistance to myxomatosis are beginning to multiply. Scientists are working on new approaches, breeding stronger viruses and other means of spreading them (such as fleas). They are also exploring the possibility of using artificial chemicals resembling the rabbits' chin scents to ring the farms and grazing lands with chemical "no-trespassing signs."

Scientists inject myxomatosis virus into a rabbit to study its effects.

Rabbits in Legend and Lore

Do you carry a rabbit's foot with you to bring you good luck? No one knows how old that practice is. Samuel Pepys, an Englishman who lived in the 1600's, mentioned in his diary that he carried a hare's foot. According to one version of the superstition, if you take the left hind foot of a rabbit into a churchyard at midnight when the moon is full, it will shield you from evil.

Lagomorph Legends

Rabbits and hares are such common animals in nearly all parts of the world that it is not surprising to find them popping up in the stories and superstitions of most peoples. South American Indians worshipped the Great Hare, which, they believed, was the creator of the universe. According to a myth of the Algonquin Indians of North

146

America, the Great Hare, Michabo, rebuilt the world after the great flood. He had gone hunting one day, and the wolves he used as hunting dogs plunged into a lake and disappeared. When Michabo went in to look for them, the lake overflowed and covered the whole world. The Great Hare asked a raven to bring him a lump of clay to remake the world, but the raven could not find any. An otter dived down, but was also unsuccessful. Finally a muskrat brought him some soil, which the Great Hare used to remake the world. Then the Great Hare married a muskmouse, and their children repopulated the world.

Hindus see the outline of a hare in the spots on the moon. Old fables of their land tell of a hare that lived on the moon and was the king of all the hares on Earth. Chinese legends, too, tell of a hare who inhabits the moon.

The Easter bunny comes from an old Teutonic legend.

According to the story, the rabbit was once a bird. Ostara, the goddess of spring, changed him into his present form. The rabbit was so grateful that he laid eggs for Ostara's spring festival (named Easter in her honor). Both rabbits, with their enormous reproductive powers, and eggs, the seeds of new life, are splendid fertility symbols for the season of spring, when life is awakening again after the long winter.

Wily Hares

The natives of Africa have many fables about hares. These small creatures are usually symbols of cleverness, and use their wits to triumph over much larger and stronger animals. In one story, for example, the hare was always borrowing from the other animals and never got around to paying them back. Finally the elephant and the hippopotamus both grew very angry with him. The hare told them that he would pay them both back with interest. Then he made a stout rope out of vines and gave one end to the elephant. "Just pull on this," he told the elephant, "and you will find a great treasure chest." Then he quickly took the other end of the rope to the hippopotamus in the river and told him the same story. The elephant and the hippo both pulled as hard as they could while the hare ran back and forth to cheer them on. Finally the elephant got thirsty and went to the river for a drink. There he met the hippo and they discovered the hare's trick. They both turned on the hare, but he ran off, laughing as he went.

148

In another African tale, there was once a time of great drought. The animals decided to cut off the tips of their ears and sell the fat from them to buy hoes to dig a well. But the hare hid himself and did not cut his ears. After the animals dug their well the hare came to drink from it, and then he washed himself and dirtied the water. The animals were so angry at this that they decided to teach the hare a lesson. They made a figure of a girl and covered it with sticky gum. The hare came along and touched the figure, then found that his paw was stuck to it. He pushed and tugged and kicked, but only succeeded in getting himself stuck tighter. The animals beat him and drove him away, and that is why the hare lives in the grasslands and has the longest ears of all the animals.

Uncle Remus Tales

In some ways this story sounds similar to the tar baby tale of Uncle Remus, and this is no coincidence. The Africans who were brought to America as slaves carried their tales with them. In their new home they found new animals and changed the stories to suit them. The hare became a cottontail rabbit. His arch-enemy, the hyena, became Br'er Fox, and the elephant became the bear. The tar baby story of Uncle Remus has a somewhat different ending, which emphasizes the habits of the cottontail. After Br'er Rabbit was caught by the tar baby, Br'er Fox carried him off, kicking and screaming, with a vow to kill him as painfully as possible. Bre'er Fox thought of hanging him or drown-

ing him or skinning him alive. To each idea, the rabbit
shrewdly replied, "Anything you want, Br'er Fox, but just
don't throw me in the brier patch." Of course that is what
the fox finally decided to do, and the rabbit ran off, chuck-
ling.

Br'er Rabbit meets the tar baby.

Another African fable is the tale of the hare and the tortoise. The tortoise challenged the hare to a race. The hare was sure he would win, but the tortoise got together all his relatives and stationed them at various points along the road. All the tortoises looked alike to the hare, and he couldn't believe that no matter how hard he ran, the tortoise was always ahead of him.

Aesop's Fables

The ancient storyteller Aesop also had a fable about the tortoise and the hare. In his version, the tortoise won the race in a different way. When they started the race, the hare bounded off, while the tortoise just plodded on in his slow and steady way. Soon the hare was so far ahead that he decided to take a rest. He fell asleep, and while he lay there the tortoise passed him and plodded on to finish line to win the race.

Aesop told a number of stories about hares and used each to point out a moral. In one story, a hare had so many friends in the forest and field that she thought she was the most popular animal of all. One day she heard hounds coming after her. She asked the horse to carry her away on his back. But the horse was too busy to help. The bull had more pressing things to do also, as did the goat, the ram, the calf, the pig, and the donkey. Finally, the hare had to take to her heels to escape the hounds. The moral that Aesop drew from this tale was, "He who has many friends has no friends."

More Famous Rabbits

All through the ages, rabbits and hares have played important roles in the tales of storytellers. In *Alice in Wonderland,* the heroine enters a fantastic world by following a white rabbit down a rabbit hole. All through the story she keeps catching glimpses of the rabbit, as he leads her from one curious adventure to another. At the Mad Hatter's tea party, she meets another lagomorph, the March Hare, who is just as mad as the hatter.

Alice at the Mad Hatter's tea party.

Mother Rabbit with Flopsy, Mopsy, Cottontail, and Peter.

One of the most famous of all the rabbit stories is Beatrix Potter's *The Tale of Peter Rabbit*. This is a simple story of a cottontail rabbit named Peter, who disobeys his mother and strays into Mr. McGregor's garden. He has a wonderful time munching on the vegetables, but then Mr. McGregor almost catches him. Peter has a series of narrow escapes and loses his new blue jacket with brass buttons, but he finally arrives home safe with his mother and three sisters, Flopsy, Mopsy, and Cottontail. Although the story is written as a fantasy, it follows the life and habits of the cottontail rabbits quite well. In this story, as in so many others, children can identify with the rabbits, as a symbol of the weak and timid triumphing in the end over the strong powers that threaten them.

153

Suggestions for Further Reading

Raising Rabbits

American Rabbit Breeders Association, Inc. *Official Guide to Raising Better Rabbits*. American Rabbit Breeders Association, Pittsburgh, Pa., 1972.

Casady, R.B., P.B. Sawin, and J. Van Dam, *Commercial Rabbit Raising*, Agriculture Handbook No. 309, U.S. Department of Agriculture, Washington, D.C., 1971.

Cooper, Elinor, *Charming Rabbits*. T.F.H. Publications, Jersey City, N. J., 1966.

Miller, Madeline, *Bunnies as Pets*. T. F. H. Publications, Jersey City, N. J., 1955.

Schneider, Earl, Editor, *Enjoy Your Rabbit*. The Pet Library, Ltd., New York.

Countryside and Small Stock Journal, Marshall, Wisconsin (magazine).

154

Natural History

Cahalane, Victor H., *Mammals of North America*. Macmillan, New York, 1961, chapter 18.

Lockley, R. M., *The Private Life of the Rabbit*. Andre Deutsch, Ltd., London, 1964.

Rue, Leonard Lee, III, *Pictorial Guide to the Mammals of North America*. Thomas Y. Crowell Co., New York, 1967, chapter 4.

Index